Born in 1945, Nick R... borders of Kent and S...

Following several nondescript jobs, which reinforced his belief that there was much more to life than his experience as an employee at the time, he set about trying to run businesses on his own account. Some were more successful than others.

This book's about the characters he met in his first meaningful and successful business, running a rural village pub which he undertook at the age of 30 and which was written as a result of what he describes as 'a triumph over adversity'. He gives no explanation for this comment.

Since the book was written, Nick has enjoyed a very successful career internationally as a senior manager for major pharmaceutical companies and has worked in South Asia, based in Taiwan for nearly nine years. He's threatening to write a book about those experiences!

Nick and Jane having now celebrated more than 32 years of marriage share their home with two Border Collies and a tabby cat in rural Surrey.

Nick Roberts is a pseudonym.

THE INN THING

A Funny Way to Run a Pub

NICK ROBERTS

TAGMAN

THE INN THING

First published in Great Britain in the year 2003 by
The Tagman Press, an imprint of Tagman Worldwide Ltd.,
Lovemore House, PO Box 754, Norwich, Norfolk NR1 4GY, England
1888 Century Park East, Suite 1900, Los Angeles CA 90067-1702, USA
www.tagman-press.com
E-mail:editorial@tagman-press.com

A Tagman Crown Laurel book

© 2003 Nick Roberts

The right of Nick Roberts to be identified as the author of this work has been asserted by him in accordance with the Copyright, Designs and Patents Act 1988

All rights reserved. No part of this publication may be reproduced, stored in a retrieval system or transmitted in any form or by any means, electronic, mechanical, recording or otherwise, without the prior written permission of the author and copyright holder.

ISBN: 1-903571-16-2

A CIP catalogue record for this book is
available from The British library

Cover & Illustrations by: Bob Allen
Typography: Malcolm Mitchell
Set in Times New Roman and Apple Chancery
Printed by: LSL Ltd

TAGMAN

Dedicated to

Crossroads

The M.S.Society

and especially to our late very dear friends

Peter & Muriel Carr
who endured life's worst abuses with
dignity and pride through the happiness
that they found together. God Bless them!

CONTENTS

Introduction: A Friend Indeed?	9
What a Birthday!	15
The Three Wise Men	23
A Green and Pleasant Land	35
Ugliness is Only Skin Deep	45
A Cold and Draughty Place	51
It Could Only Get Better!	61
Below the Bar	67
Great Groats! Blessed Beer!	77
The Domino Factor	83
Things that Go Bump in the Night	93
Wakey Wakey... Rise and Shine!	99
Tact and Diplomacy	111
A Funny Way to Run a Pub	127
Feather, Fur and Folklore	153
Behind the Bar	175
Crime and Disaster	209
Last Orders!	227

Introduction:
A Friend Indeed?

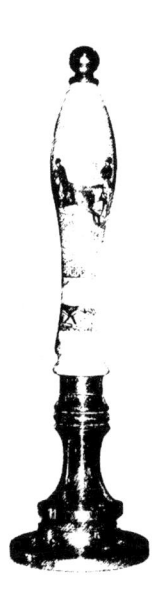

Being the Tenant, Manager or Owner of a public house is a fraught affair as any of those unfortunates that you happen to know behind the bar will be willing to tell you if you have the courage to broach the subject.

The difficulties start long before you pull your first pint!

Any Landlord who disagrees with this premise is either a consummate liar, somebody worthy of certifying under the Mental Health Act or an alien just arrived from a planet of which we've never heard.

Back in the mid-70s, Jane and I had made the fateful decision to take over a pub in a remote village in Northamptonshire and in this book, we hope to give you a flavour of what's involved in pursuing this way of life.

In order to obtain the all important Justices Licence as a fit and proper person to run Licensed premises, you had to obtain references from various sources including friends who had known you for several years.

I've given below an example of one such a letter (including what I can only assume to be intentional spelling mistakes and a complete misjudgment of our characters), which was purportedly sent to the Court. (Friends like this you do not need!):

To the Majistrates.

I have known my friend Mr Roberts for about 10 years and consider him to be a fit and proper person to hold a Justises Licence.

I have found him to be entirely honest and trust-worthy and he can be relied upon to do anybody... a good turn. He's entirely at home in any public house and quickly learns the geography of each one especially the positions of such vital objects as the gentlemen's toilets, the till and the Best Bitter pump!

He would always be ready to learn by accepting tips from his customers and would never offend his clientele by closing on time just to be able to go to bed and would work well into the night if asked by his customers.

After all, this is what he has demanded of every Landlord whose pub he has visited.

He's very confident of his own abilities, even more when he's (pissed and) enjoying his work and natural calling.

I, like Mr Roberts, know very little about his financial affairs, but they must be in very good order as he has had many affairs to date. He was once a Greengrocer and was known locally as the local swede (I know of no foreign blood though).

He's dilligent and hard werking, always when flat out on the job and I would imagine that he would keep the structure of his premises in good (Nick) repair as he says he pays a lot of attention to paying for maintenance and has spent a lot of time on the tiles.

The regular clientele would be more than doubled by Mr Robert's present drinking company and I am sure that there are hundreds of others who would love to know where they could find him.

I know from personal experience that his wife would keep a very good house at a reasonable cost and is extremely experienced at handling the customers.

Mr Roberts has always felt a (knee) need to be a licencee as he has always said to me about his barmaid: 'She needs a job', 'One day I'll give her one'.

He's a very able salesman and, in his present occupation, apparently in the pharmaceutical industry, would sell drugs to anyone, anywhere, at any price.

Two years ago, his efforts were acknowledged by his firm when he shared, with another salesman their top award, The Farr Cup. This year he distinguished himself by single handedly achieving a complete Farr Cup in his own right. What a Farr Cup that was!

To sum up; Mr Roberts is basically gentle... In fact he's quite light fingered and healthy; I have never known him to be queer and he's also very attentive to other peoples' problems. He will always sort anyone out with or without provocation, in fact, he likes nothing more than a good punch-up in a pub especially after closing time.

I have no hesitation in recommending him as a suitable person for whatever judgement The Court decides.

Yours at her Majesty's pleasure.

Alexander the Grate.
Broadmoor.'

This close and dear friend never showed me a copy of the real letter which he had sent to the Court, but I can only assume that it was nothing like the one above otherwise I would've been rejected without sight knowing the sense of humour at large in those days.

What a Birthday!

11.00am, October 14th 1975. I remember the date well because it was my 30th birthday, and I suppose to some extent it was the reminder of advancing years that prompted me into realising one of my ambitions; To be the landlord of a country inn.

For the first time in my life, I stood in the dock of a magistrates court, feeling for all the world like a criminal, but for no other reason than to receive the court's approval that I was a fit and proper person to hold a licence to sell intoxicating liquors.

The police inspector was asked if he had any objections to the court's approval, and I waited with baited breath for his reply.

Thoughts flashed through my mind about the time when, as a lad, I had been cheeky to a motor-cycle policeman when he stopped me for carrying a passenger on the crossbar of my bicycle. I had received a clip around the ear for that crime and another from my father when I was escorted home.

'No objections your Honour,' replied the Inspector. 'Licence granted,' said the chairman of the bench, and I was led away from the dock by a court official feeling as though I was about to start a sentence for my misdemeanours.

Outside in the bright Autumn sunshine, I spoke with one of the young policemen on court duty that day and we laughed about my guilty feelings. His name was Ron and we were to become firm friends over the next few years. At the time, I had no idea that my pub was part of his beat and that he could either have been my guardian angel or my worst enemy. It's a sad reflection that at that time, many policemen had few friends outside the force so when I invited him to visit our new hostelry together with his wife for our opening party, he readily accepted.

12.30pm, October 14th 1975. I walked through the front door as the legal tenant landlord of the 'Dog and Partridge' in the tiny village of Mearsby which nestled in the rolling countryside of the Nene Valley in Northamptonshire.

Awaiting my arrival was my wife Jane, her parents, one local by the name of Wilf of whom you will hear much more and to my surprise, the Managing Director of Ruddles Brewery, Mr Tony Ruddle accompanied by his Estates Director who had first interviewed us as potential licensees.

Wilf's first comment was: 'I hope yers not gonna be this bloody late opening every day... Mine's a mild and bitter.'

Tony Ruddle was the perfect gentleman and paid for every drink that was served during our opening lunchtime session.

The first day in a new pub is a fraught affair. Not only are you moving house but you negotiate with the outgoing landlord on the value of the contents of the house, agree on stock valuation and complete the legal formalities whilst trying to run the business.

Our plan was simple. I was to run the bar whilst Jane and her parents supervised the unloading and placing of our furniture. This was complicated by the irrepressible nature of our English Setter, Houdini and the total lack of cooperation of our two cats Monty and Barney who insisted on trying to terrorise our pet rabbit Flopsy to the extent that all the animals had to be incarcerated in separate rooms making furniture placing all but impossible.

The lunchtime session ended with a telephone call from my solicitor advising that completion of the sale of our house had been delayed for a week or so. This was awkward to say the least since funds from the house sale were all I had to pay the brewery and outgoing tenant. Fortunately I had a good relationship with the Manager of my Barclay's branch and one telephone call was all it took for him to agree for me to write the necessary cheques in order to finally take over the tenancy.

It's interesting to note that the bank never made a service charge nor an interest charge for arranging the impromptu loan or for the three weeks which it took to repay. I can't help wondering what would happen in the same circumstances today.

What with all the chaos, the afternoon flew past and before we knew it, evening opening time had arrived.

Our furniture was still in all the wrong places, none of the fires had been lit, the lunchtime glasses were still waiting to be washed, the animals were screaming for food as indeed were we when the first trickle of customers appeared.

To be honest, I do not recall too much detail of that first night behind the bar except that both the bitter and lager barrels ran out within a few minutes of each other causing me some panic as for the first time in my life, I had to wrestle with beer lines and carbon dioxide cylinders whilst trying to remember the sequence of connections.

Apart from the odd complaint about the price of bitter

being an exorbitant 18p a pint, the evening went smoothly enough, more due to the good nature of our customers than to any barmanship skills on my part.

At long last, the session came to an end and I wearily called time thinking of nothing more than a good night's sleep. Most of the people left wishing us good luck with some stressing that we'd need it but three locals steadfastly remained seated.

'Yers a bit sharp on time aren't yers?' queried Wilf of the Mild and Bitter. 'Previous Landlord used ter stay open fer us fer at least two more!'

I was about to reply when two uniformed policemen entered the bar. 'Come on then. Drink up and go home. You've got two minutes to leave... Landlord you stay where you are, we want a word with you!'

The three locals downed their drinks and with a total lack of grace, left muttering something about a police state.

The constables approached the bar, removing their hats as they did so. 'Couldn't have them keeping you up half the night on your first day so to speak, now could we,' smirked Ron. 'So how about two unofficial pints for me and Cyril and a chance to meet your family?'

To be fair to them, they offered to pay for their drinks but I had the feeling deep down that this was a glorious opportunity to build a deep meaningful relationship with our defenders and protectors. In any event it would've been illegal to charge them after hours! When they had gone, Jane served my birthday dinner of cheese and onion sandwiches having saved a few from those we had supplied our customers. Then came the bombshell! There hadn't been time to put together our beds, let alone put them in the right rooms so we simply dragged mattresses into the bar room, curled up in sleeping bags and slept together with the in-laws and the animals except for the rabbit of course who by now was safely ensconced in her personal quarters. I can't help thinking that she was the most comfortable of all of us.

During the night we made a discovery. The bar room was infested with mice but their numbers were somewhat reduced by the morning as a result of Monty and Barney's attentions. The only person who slept that night was May, Jane's mother and just as well too since she goes into a catatonic state at the very mention of our small furry friends.

For the first time in their lives, the cats were going to earn their living. It was a very large, very old and very dilapidated building. The perfect habitat for all manner of wildlife, not all of whom were welcome guests.

The Three Wise Men

In virtually every rural pub in Great Britain, you will almost certainly find an outstanding local character. A man to whom regulars and visitors alike will be drawn to hear colourful stories of days gone by. A man for whom drinks will be readily bought in return for his most outrageous tales and grossest exaggerations.

We, for our sins, had three of these entertaining old rogues whose sharp intellect was disguised only by their advanced years and rustic appearance but who, in their serious moments, would let pearls of wisdom fall from their lips as quickly as raindrops in an April shower.

In their own environment as true countrymen, they were magnificent. Throughout this book you will hear of their exploits. They were Wilf, George and Enoch. All lived within staggering distance of the Dog and Partridge and treated our pub as their second home and both of us as part of their families. They were the greatest of friends whilst being the strongest of rivals but no matter the heat of their arguments, they remained the closest band of old gentlemen I have ever had the pleasure to know.

George, the youngest of the three, was in his mid-60s and still worked full time as head stockman at one of the two farms surrounding the village. Despite his title, he was responsible for just about everything to do with running the farm on a day to day basis. His boss, Mr Brent was the owner of the farm which had been in his family for centuries and despite running the business efficiently and at a profit, insisted on conservation of his land as a major priority. He couldn't have found a better person than George to be his top man for both doing the work and training the younger farm workers.

Stocky, ruddy faced and eternally optimistic, George was the very epitome of the countryman. He lived with his wife Mabel in a tied cottage belonging to Mr Brent and promoted the simple philosophy that if you had enough to eat and drink, had no debts, a roof over your head and were in good health, then you were a rich man indeed.

Born, bred and schooled in Mearsby, George had never strayed far from the village except with little choice in the Second World War; an episode in his life of which he never spoke. This subject was closed to all and we could only guess at the experiences which he had endured. Perhaps it was his natural desire to find goodness in all things that had shut that period away for ever. We shall never know.

He was a great authority on animals both wild and domestic and was totally at one with the countryside. Had he been given the opportunity of a better basic education, he would've made a fine veterinary surgeon. He was a born naturalist and would talk for hours about the local flora and fauna with an enthusiasm that was spellbinding.

Except for Sundays, he rarely changed his dress style. He was nearly always to be seen wearing his flat tweed cap in winter or summer, a dark blue boiler suit and heavy black Wellington boots. His only concession to the coldest and wettest of the winter weather was a scarf which had been knitted decades previously by Mabel and an even older oversized raincoat, tied around the middle with a piece of baler twine.

His Sunday best clothes, apart from the rare occasions when he went to church, would be corduroy trousers, thick open necked flannel shirt and a sleeveless woollen pullover. He always removed his cap on entering a house, including our pub.

He was the mildest mannered of men, having a smile for everybody and the most infuriating ability to find something good in the most disastrous situations.

Until you got to know him, he appeared to be a bumbling, slow and rather dull witted individual but beneath that rustic exterior lay a razor sharp wit, a clever sense of humour and an understanding of the human condition to which many a professor of psychology would aspire.

His favourite expression was: 'It'll be orlright, you'll see... It'll be orlright'.

No matter the problem, if anybody asked him to explain how it could be 'orlright', he was always able to give a sensible answer. We certainly never found him wanting for a reply.

By contrast, Wilf, who was by now in his 80s was a gruff, if not to say a miserable old moaner but nevertheless managed to find his way into the affections of people who took the trouble to get to know him.

He had a giant chip on his shoulder which I understand was related to his being retired from full time farm work at the age of 80 by Mr Brent. He still enjoyed the use of his tied cottage free of charge, free of rates, free of any maintenance costs and free of any electricity or gas bills. Mr Brent paid all of these and even paid him a 'pension' in return for visiting the farm for an hour three times a week to advise on the continued good running of the business.

Despite this he felt that he had been cast aside in his prime and that youngsters like George had usurped his position.

Wilf had a permanently angry look on his face which was accentuated by a fearsome walrus moustache which covered his entire mouth. It was impossible to say whether he ever smiled. Rumour has it that he did from time to time but only Wilf would ever have known for sure.

Like George, Wilf had spent his entire life in and around Mearsby but unlike George, rarely had a good word for anybody; especially those better off than he was which meant just about everybody.

Fiercely proud of his status as the oldest active member of the community, he liked to be the centre of attraction at any gathering at the Dog and Partridge but his rather sour attitude to life meant that many of the younger locals would avoid him. This was a pity because given sufficient ale, he could be very amusing.

On the other hand, his peers took fiendish delight in provoking him into his customary angry outbursts.

I wouldn't say that he was paranoid, but, he held one strong belief of which he would never tire of telling anyone willing to buy him a pint and listen.

Namely, that the introduction of mixamatosis in the 50s to control the rabbit population was in fact a conspiracy by the well heeled ruling classes to stop poor country folk from obtaining their meat for nothing. This was to keep them totally dependent on their employers for their existence and to 'keep them in their place'.

Despite his constant grumbling, he was a real character

and the Dog and Partridge would've been much the poorer without him.

Our most unforgettable character was Enoch — aptly named in consideration of his extreme right-wing views on politics — contradicted by his almost communistic views on the distribution of wealth. He was a complicated man who loved nothing more than a lively debate and could hold forth on any subject.

A Yorkshireman by birth, he spent his formative years in the Yorkshire Dales where, as he never ceased to tell us: 'Yers 'ave t' be tough t' survive'.

Since the end of the Second World War, he had lived in Mearsby with his wife Edna and had raised a large family of four daughters and a son Jim, who still lived in the village working on Mr Ford's farm.

Enoch was well into his 70s and had long since retired from paid employment but all his days were spent beavering away with astonishing energy and resolution which many men half his age would've found difficult to equal.

Always dressed in a pork pie hat, tweed jacket with leather elbow patches, moleskin trousers and heavy brown brogues, he could be seen working with a will except of course during pub opening hours.

His working life, if his stories were to be believed was amazingly varied. His vast experience which produced his never ending fund of stories had included the following occupations:

Coal Miner
Blacksmith

Farrier (is there a difference?)
Water engineer
RSM — Yorkshire Regiment
Grave digger
Cavalryman
Horse breeder
Farm worker
Golf club maker
Publican

and no doubt many other worthy occupations about which he didn't volunteer any information.

His daily toils were directed into three main tasks; Poultry-keeping, vegetable growing and wood cutting. He kept on average, 20 laying hens and a handful of raucous cockerels who had no respect for Sunday mornings and ensured that oversleeping wasn't a characteristic of Mearsby folk.

Each hen, he maintained, would lay upwards of 300 eggs per year. Given an annual output of some 6,000 eggs, you do not have to be a genius to realise that he and his dear wife Edna couldn't have possibly consumed that quantity and still remained perfectly healthy.

The crops which he grew on his half acre allotment had to be seen to be believed. Sufficient to feed at least a dozen people during the growing season and from storage during the long cold winter months.

I do not think that there was anything that he couldn't grow successfully and of a quality which would make many a high class greengrocer blush with shame. We were presented with bundles of crisp spring onions during

December. How he grew them so well at that time of year, I do not know but they were excellent.

When he wasn't tending his garden or his poultry, he could be seen bent over a trestle, busily guiding his bow saw through branches of Elm wood which grew in plenty in and around the village. Many was the time when he would be seen trudging back from a walk in the meadows or Mearsby copse, his back straining under the burden of dead wood ripped from the trees by the prevailing North Easterly wind which was a constant companion during the Winter period.

He would say: 'Never come back from a walk empty handed', and he for one never did.

You would be forgiven for thinking that Enoch had a thriving business marketing his produce but this wasn't the case. The only time I ever knew him to actually sell his goods was when he provided one of our friends with point-of-lay pullets and only then would accept payment when the birds had produced their first eggs.

He and Edna lived on their state pension and his Army pension, catering for many of their needs from the garden and poultry-house produce, the balance of which went to people in the village who were unable for one reason or another to provide for themselves. All this went on season after season without fuss and without the knowledge of many of the area's quite well off people. Most of these people couldn't have begun to understand that Enoch's hard labour wasn't financially motivated.

You can see that Enoch was far from being a mean man, however, during October he had discovered a rich source of wild mushrooms, the whereabouts of which, he kept very much to himself. Not once did he give any clues which was rather surprising as he was a mischievous character, who at times, would delight in misleading people just for the fun of it.

Early every morning, Enoch would be seen returning from his foray into the secret mushroom place, his wicker basket brimming with dew fresh, succulent mushrooms. Many people tackled him on the subject but none succeeded with the exception of Mr Fyffe, whose cottage on the outskirts of the village, Enoch would pass carrying his freshly picked fruits of the earth.

Now, Mr Fyffe wasn't the most popular man at Mearsby. Not that he had ever done anything to deserve being disliked. He simply kept himself to himself and rarely made contact with the villagers presumably because he had little in common with them and preferred his own company. This led the locals to believe that he was snobbish in outlook.

One evening, Enoch gave him directions to the hallowed and secret mushroom patch.

The following morning, off went Mr Fyffe carrying a basket of the type which bakers' roundsmen used to deliver our daily bread. It was enormous; about three feet long, two feet wide and 18 inches deep. Why on earth he wanted that many mushrooms was something at which we could only guess but I suspect that it wasn't for the same altruistic reasons as for Enoch's daily toil.

Mr Fyffe returned about two hours later, slightly worse for wear after his journey, which on Enoch's advice had taken him through Mearsby Copse, a very dense thicket made almost impenetrable by gorse and briar. He had understood from Enoch that some of the mushrooms were in a clearing. From the Copse he'd had to cross an open meadow inhabited by a herd of inquisitive, if not to say aggressive bullocks, over an unbridged stream and finally into a pasture bordered by the River Nene.

For his pains he had managed to gather not more than one pound of mushrooms.

On hearing this, Enoch broke into a wide smirk of satisfaction, his twinkling blue eyes flashing with triumph. 'By the left!' he laughed. 'Someone must 'ave got there before 'im, the greedy owd bugger.'

Months later Enoch admitted that he had sent poor old Fyffe on a wild goose chase with the words: 'Ah knew 'e'd 'ave t'bloddy well work fer 'is mushrooms if 'e went bah t'bloddy copse.'

His Yorkshire accent always became more pronounced after a few drinks.

A Green and Pleasant Land

The countryside of the Nene Valley isn't very spectacular, but beautiful it most certainly is.

There are no ravines or deep gorges, no natural waterfalls and no high hilltop views to take your breath away. But there are gentle hills bounded by the slow moving silver ribbons of the River Nene and its tributaries. Forests of pine, mixed deciduous woods, spinneys and copses are to be seen in any direction and the meadows and pastures in the Spring time are so lush and green, it wouldn't be fanciful to think that the sheep and cattle step lightly to avoid damaging the rich carpet of grass and clover which also sustains them.

Hedgerows of mixed thorns, elder, wild rose and blackberry to name but a few, are neatly kept and, flowering right through the Spring and Summer, form a picture postcard border between the fields and pastures, marking, as they have for centuries, the extent of individual ownership of land and other rural boundaries.

They provide a sanctuary and habitat for wildlife which, if you're prepared to look for it, display a kaleidoscope of natural variety.

There were hedgerows in abundance in our part of Northamptonshire and I am sure that it was these which helped to account for the many different species of birds and mammals to be found. Rarities such as the Little owl and the Red squirrel were frequently sighted, not in large numbers but nevertheless successfully holding their own.

Making comparisons with the Fenland further East where hedgerows had been systematically grubbed out to provide huge plains for cereal growing, you would've noticed a definite lack of wildlife. At the time, it was felt no doubt that food production was far more important than a few miles of hedgerow but if the perpetrators had stopped to consider that every creature from the lowliest insect to the larger mammals all play an important part in the balance of nature and that crop development was an integral part of that balance, then they'd have realised that hedge removal was a gross interference in the natural scheme of things. The short term gains in increased crop production were marginalised when Nature made her redress. The draught was literally felt in parts of East Anglia when the wind, unbroken by hedgerows, carried off the valuable topsoil so necessary to the crop production which was supposed to have been boosted by removing the hedges.

We were extremely lucky and pleased that the Northamptonshire farmers and landowners were conservationist in outlook and it's due to them and their efforts that our countryside and scenery has changed so little over the years.

Some of our fondest memories of Mearsby are of the beautiful country views which could be seen from every upstairs window at the pub.

I think my favourite view was to the South across the meadow where a herd of Friesian dairy cows lazily grazed and beyond to a large pond surrounded by rushes and willows together with half a dozen once proud elm trees which sadly were beginning to show the ravages of the tragedy known as Dutch elm disease.

To the far right of the pond was a solid Northamptonshire

stone farmhouse which had stood unchanged for four centuries flanked by an eight foot high dry stone wall which curved gently away to the right being part of and marking for all to see, the original boundary of Mearsby.

In the early Spring, before the grass became really thick, we could clearly see, in a different shade of green, the ground on which the ancient settlement of Mearsby had stood. The area was so clearly marked with tracks, roadways and places where buildings had once been built that with a little imagination, we could almost see the village as it once was.

A little further to the right and bordered by an ivy covered stone wall running alongside the lane, the meadow swept gently upwards towards Mearsby Copse which in the Autumn, was a splendid riot of green, gold, yellow, red and brown especially when it caught the dying rays of the setting sun still further to the right and just out of view.

Looking carefully towards the pond, we'd often see a grey heron in the shallows, standing on one leg, perfectly still, watching the progress of an unwary fish as yet out of range until suddenly, with a movement almost too fast to see, the head and neck would drop into the water and the unfortunate fish would become a snack.

The heron is one of the better fishermen in the Nene Valley; he rarely if ever misses a bite.

Beyond the pond, a thorn hedge marked the boundary between the meadow and Mr Ford's pasture which sloped gently away and down towards the river which was just out of sight. Looking further to the south on the other side of the river, a panorama of patchwork fields, their colours blending, climbed softly towards the horizon which was broken by the hazy outline of woodland and the occasional isolated stone building.

To the left of the meadow and virtually opposite our pub was a lane which ran past four traditional stone cottages and was separated from them by an ivy clad stone wall. The lane led to our tiny church whose origins were shrouded in the mists of time, such was its age.

At the end of the lane was a pair of massive iron gates, always open, beyond which was a tree and shrub lined drive leading to a magnificent 17th century rectory whose imposing size and surrounding elm trees obscured any more of the view in that direction.

That was the scene that we found so captivating to look at but so much more fascinating to walk in.

Contrary to popular opinion, a publican does not have a great deal of spare time and our one big regret was that we were unable to spend longer periods out and about in the countryside. However, Sunday afternoons were usually free and whenever possible, accompanied by Houdini, we'd set off towards the river.

One afternoon we came across George laying a hedge in Mr Ford's pasture. It was a treat to watch this highly skilled countryman at work but oh so slowly. Effortlessly, he swung his sharp bill hook, not to sever but to cut only part way through the boughs so that they could be bent over and entwined with the branches of the neighbouring bush to form a continuous hedge which would also act as a fence to stop the sheep from straying.

'You'll have to work faster than that George,' I teased. 'Or you'll get the sack.'

'No fear o' tha' boy,' he cackled. 'Yers doan 'ave ter rush ter do a job quickly. Yous 'jes wait an see.'

We left him to his labours and made for the stile which led to the little used footpath running behind the Rectory and eventually meeting the farm track which would take us down to the river. The path itself was a thick carpet of grass flanked on either side by wild rose and blackberry bushes. Here and there, under the hedges, were outcrops of wild pea and tiny wild orchids which owed their survival to the seclusion of the environment. Above was a swaying canopy of green where the large elms which skirted the path interwove their topmost limbs with each other and the occasional majestic oak to form a natural shady tunnel.

Now and then, a rabbit would dart across the path making for its refuge in a hollow tree or amongst the roots and stems of the briars. Many rabbits were living above ground, having abandoned their warrens as a natural defence against the scourge of mixamatosis. The disease was still making its presence felt in the County and it was very sad to see so many half crippled and blind animals struggling in a hopeless effort for survival.

Stopping for a moment, we heard the intermittent stacatto sound of a Greater Spotted Woodpecker busily drilling a tree although we were unable to catch a sight of him.

Leaving the footpath, we turned onto the farm track and into the open countryside. The stillness was dramatic; so peaceful yet at the same time alive with creatures going about their daily business. A Grey Heron wheeled overhead seeming to steer his graceful passage through the sky by using his long trailing legs as directional rudders. A hare raced across the open field on our left, rushing madly at breakneck speed as if in flight from some unseen enemy whilst rabbits, pheasant and partridge, disturbed by Houdini's quartering, dashed this way and that to avoid him.

There below us was the river, lazily meandering like a shimmering silver ribbon through the valley. This was the home of countless waterfowl, the playground of anglers and boaters and most importantly, the giver of life and fertility to the verdant green pastures through which it flowed.

We were lucky enough to spot a Coot's nest in a still backwater and actually watch the young hatchlings emerge from the eggs. To our surprise, whilst the mother fussed about them, the youngsters, only minutes old, plunged straight into the water and were swimming immediately with the greatest of ease whilst peeping excitedly at their new found freedom.

Lost in its natural splendour and quite alone apart from the birds and animals, we strolled alongside the river where common bream would, from time to time, rise slowly to the surface and lazily roll over, their flanks reflecting the bright sunlight before diving to the bottom. Mallard and Moorhens fussed noisily in the rushes and reeds for food. Suddenly, a brilliant flash of blue and orange swooped from a willow tree, following the river course at water level then veered off into the rushes on the opposite bank. It was a Kingfisher, something of a rarity but obviously existing happily in the valley.

We followed the same route that we had taken to the river to return home and three hours after we had set out, George was just packing his equipment at the end of his day. To our surprise, the hedge was completed. 'I told yers,' he smirked. 'Yers doan 'ave ter rush ter do a job quickly.'

Mearsby itself was a tiny village. The main road which was little more than a lane was flanked on both sides by the tied cottages belonging to Mr Ford and Mr Brent. There was the dear old Dog and Partridge and the church.

Less than 50 people lived there but that certainly didn't stop it from being one of the most interesting and friendly communities in which we've ever had the pleasure to live.

Ugliness is Only Skin Deep

When we first moved to the Dog and Partridge it really didn't rate very highly as a commercial proposition, especially as it was situated in a tiny village with a small local patronage and on a road which basically went from nowhere to nowhere. We didn't have the funds to take over a pub that was doing well, but always felt that with the right approach, we could transform the place into a comfortable and popular watering hole.

Whilst we never intended it to make our fortune, the pub had to support us and preserve the savings and proceeds from the sale of our house which had been invested in it.

Our view, as somewhat accomplished supporters of other peoples' pubs, was that to sell drinks on a sufficient scale to provide our living, we had to offer a warm, comfortable, welcoming pub which retained the olde worlde atmosphere of a 400 year old country house.

You would've thought that such an old building would've been full of character. After all, at the time it was built, Henry VIII was having his merry way throughout the land and generally setting the scene for Britain to become Great.

Alas, the building, at least on the inside didn't live up to its historical beginnings so we decided to strip away the centuries of abuse and insult that had been heaped upon it by previous owners and tenants.

Constructed in Northamptonshire stone with walls six feet thick and roofed with ancient Collyweston slate tiles, the Dog and Partridge was a most handsome and imposing survivor of Old Mearsby. Unfortunately, on entering the building it became clear that strenuous efforts had been made to bury any charm that the interior had once offered.

As a listed building of course, it wasn't possible to make 'modern improvements', but successive occupants had done their best to destroy its character with gallons of paint and the uninhibited use of plywood and plastic laminates.

We knew that beneath this desecration, lay a charm that once uncovered, would be captivating, warm and welcoming.

We also knew that one of the previous landlords had been interested in pig keeping but the state of the place suggested that he kept his animals in the bar when the pub was closed and in the back room cellar during opening hours.

Our assumption turned out to be wrong but all will be revealed about the pigs in due course.

It wouldn't be fair to say that the place was dirty as such but neglected, tatty and abused would be a more appropriate description.

The centuries old oak beams which supported the ground floor ceilings, had, presumably in Victorian times been boxed in with some rather cheap and nasty panelling. At a later date, this had been covered with plywood and painted black. These coverings were split, crumbling, worm infested and about as attractive as a rusty steel joist.

The paper covering the walls and ceiling, once white, had taken on the appearance of recycled French toilet tissue and was peeling away from the surfaces in more places than where it was firmly stuck.

Ventilation was provided by the open windows... Open at all times since the lack of maintenance over the years had warped both the frames and the casements.

  Where the windows would close, there were cracked and broken panes and where the glass was intact the casements refused to match the frames.

A Cold and Draughty Place!

To our mind, the greatest crime of all was the paint-work. What had once been beautiful pine panelled doors and a pine panelled screen wall fronted by a several centuries old oak monks' settle had all been coated variously with heavy oil based green and cream gloss paint. The surfaces were so filmed that it was difficult to tell the difference between the colours.

This paint resisted all attempts to remove it without damaging the beautiful wood over which it had been daubed.

Hanging from the ceiling were wartime pendant lamps, some of which were broken, containing high power bulbs which illuminated the depressing scene.

The huge inglenook fireplace had been carefully blocked with cheap plywood tables surrounded by black vinyl covered tubular steel chairs. Similar chairs also lined the walls along with various broken tables in a manner which would've done justice to the ideas of a late 19th century railway waiting room planner.

To complete the awful scene, heavy curtains of an indeterminate shape and colour fought an uneven battle with the gale howling through the broken windows whilst a dart board had been nailed to the longest wall in such a position that the room was effectively cut in half whilst play was in progress.

An elderly juke-box blared out previous years' forgotten pop songs and an even more elderly fruit machine eagerly snatched the loose change from those foolhardy enough to chance their luck, not to mention their fingers when they tried to extract the coins which the machine should from time to time have returned to them.

This sorry pattern was repeated throughout the house and included seven bedrooms, all in a similar condition.

A passageway on the first floor stretched 60 feet from one end of the house to the other, connecting all the upstairs rooms together with three staircases which all needed restoration and decoration before we'd be in a position to accept a single overnight guest.

The jewel in this devastated house was the kitchen.

It was a dark, cavernous room, measuring 20 feet by 20 feet, the best part of which was its stone flagged floor.

It contained only a small, cracked porcelain sink fed by two ancient taps supported by the crumbling masonry of the wall which separated this room from the car park. Just!

On examining the room, our thoughts returned to the pigs.

Could this have been where they were kept? It certainly could have been but as things turned out, it wasn't, but as I said before, we'll come to the pigs later.

As you can see, it wasn't the most attractive country pub you could have wished to visit and it had been run on the lines of a very low grade drinking house for many years, mainly for the benefit of a darts team who, by and large, gave their support to the pub on home match nights only. On these nights, only Wilf, Enoch and George would be seen in the place and I suspect that if at the time they had enjoyed access to transport, even they'd have gone elsewhere.

On other nights, we were visited by people who we still number amongst our friends but unfortunately, the majority were characters whose disappearance from any bar would likely have been greeted with relief by patrons and landlords anywhere.

The dross from which we were earning our living would dress, by choice, and not by circumstance, in filthy boots, foul jeans and vests whose last sight of a laundry basket would've been lost in the mists of time. When sober, which wasn't for long, their language, in normal conversation was abusive but after swilling their beer, was enough to embarrass the occupants of a barrack room.

They liked their pub to look like a pigsty and treated it as such, with no respect for themselves, their surroundings or the feelings of other people who were brave enough to use the pub.

It seemed to us that we were catering for the drop outs of the County and that the main attraction was the general low condition of the bar and the availability of the dart board which was rarely used by the more pleasant visitors, presumably for fear of upsetting this crude and unpredictable crew. It transpired later that this unpleasant group of our clientele had been banned from most of the pubs within a 15 mile radius.

It was hardly surprising that the men rarely, if ever, brought their wives or girlfriends to the Dog and Partridge.

It was clear that we had to do something about our undesirable customers, and in any event, we hadn't come to the country to have our lives made miserable by a bunch of leering, abusive layabouts.

Following a particularly disastrous home darts match when tables and chairs were used as ashtrays, sandwiches were trampled into the floor and the bar looked like the terraces of Wembley in the aftermath of a home International, we withdrew from the darts league, removed the darts board and set about upgrading the entire place.

Out with the dart board went the majority of the yobs and down went our income... Drastically!

For 40 days, not to mention nights, we cleaned, scrubbed, scraped, painted and pasted.

The windows and frames were made to measure and replaced by a local builder by the name of Walter whose prodigious appetite for tea and coffee whilst working was tempered only by the number of times he had to leave his scaffold to make room for more.

One morning at about 7.30 with the frost thick on the ground, I woke with a start to see Walter climbing through our bedroom wall where he had just removed the window and frame. Jane, her long blonde hair cascading over her shoulders opened her eyes, sat up in bed, then realising that Walter was standing there, let out a yelp of surprise, burrowed under the bedclothes for cover and yelled at me in a most unladylike way to get him out.

Contriving to look embarrassed at his 'mistake' he said: 'I thought as 'ow you slept in the next room along. What'll I do now?'

More very unladylike comments came from under the blankets but were sufficiently muffled for Walter not to hear them. I sat up blinking stupidly at him and trying to shake off the dullness brought on by a good night's sleep and a rude awakening when he grinned at me. 'I reckon as 'ow I'll go an' put kettle on while yous gerrup.' It's amazing the lengths some people will go to just to get a cup of coffee.

We've never let Walter forget that incident but we are still not sure to this day whether his mistake was genuine.

Two weeks before Christmas, the bar restoration was completed and, not before time, the real character of the place had been revealed.

The oak beams had been stripped, treated and contrasted majestically against the white rough cast of the ceilings and walls. We were lucky enough to find a craftsman who was able to stain and feather grain the panelling and doors which we couldn't strip without damaging the timber. The Jacobean oak colouring must have reflected how the house had looked all those years before but it was always a source of regret to us that we were never able to restore the fabric to its original condition.

The replaced windows and frames, now crisp and clean in white gloss, sealed the room against draughts and were lit by a pair of antique ship's lamps acquired from an old fisherman on the East coast.

Other antique paraphernalia from the same marine source graced the walls and softened the starkness of the freshly painted surfaces. We were able to obtain a set of quite old prints of sailing vessels which we hung on the wooden panelling and lit the inglenook fireplace with a huge copper masthead lamp from a Lowestoft Drifter.

The ugly pendant lamps were consigned to history and replaced with low powered orange lamps between the oak beams which gave a cozy warm glow to the rough cast of the ceiling and walls.

The electric coal effect fire in the inglenook (how could they have done that?) was ousted and replaced by a blazing coal and log fire in a huge basket which not only warmed the room but created a wonderful, if sometimes smoky atmosphere.

The juke-box was retired and replaced with a hidden music system over which I had complete control of music choice and volume whilst the fruit machine was consigned to the barn outside.

The room looked great but the furniture, set against the new background, appeared even more seedy and totally out of place, spoiling the overall effect.

Digging even deeper into our limited cash reserves, we bought reproduction oak tables and chairs which we arranged in random groups throughout the room and completed the transformation with a suite of old but supremely comfortable settee and armchairs for the tired and weary to enjoy the warmth of the open fire.

At last, the main public room and indeed the adjacent small snug room were inviting places to visit, offering a cozy and friendly haven for friends to meet, eat, drink and be merry.

We now had the task of re-building the Dog and Partridge into a friendly country pub whose character and atmosphere would provide a warm and agreeable environment which would encourage people to visit us more regularly.

We wanted to provide a retreat where folk could escape from the daily mud bath of human endeavour and really enjoy themselves and their friends' company without interference from the bullying, aggressive types which the pub had previously attracted.

As it happened, our restorations and the upheaval involved had seen the departure of the remainder of our unwelcome customers but had sadly also prompted others, who we'd have liked to retain, to seek another pub.

Clearly we were not able to please everybody.

Fortunately, for our financial health, the newly attracted customers far outnumbered those which we had lost and perhaps more importantly, wives and girlfriends accompanied their men on a regular basis.

Our income began to rise steadily but we realised there was still a great deal to be done to make the Dog and Partridge the place to go.

It Could Only Get Better

Having completed the restorations, at least as far as the customers could see, we wanted to do something completely different in the way of publicity and as Christmas was just around the corner, we felt that a Carol service in the pub would be a good idea.

Our local vicar was somewhat reticent about the whole idea but when we pointed out that he would've had a better opportunity to reach a far bigger 'flock' in the pub than would attend his church, he reluctantly agreed to officiate. In any event, the service was to be in addition to that held at the church and certainly not as a competitive function.

The villagers rallied round and Mr Ford arranged for his piano to be brought to the pub on a fork lift truck. It was manhandled into a corner of the lounge by our locals.

The vicar and church wardens set to with a will and organised music and a choice of carols together with festive poetry and anecdotes.

This really was the first expression of welcome to us and a token of appreciation by the whole village for what we were trying to do. This was reinforced when Mr Ford, whose family rarely, if ever, visited the pub gave us a huge Christmas tree to help decorate the lounge. We placed one advertisement in the local newspaper under the heading 'Winter Warmer at Mearsby' with a line drawing of the inglenook and a blazing fire and an invitation to sing carols with us on December 22nd 1975 at 8.00pm.

On the evening of the big event, we waited nervously to see what would happen. We needn't have worried. By 7.30pm, the room was packed to capacity by villagers, including Mr Ford's and Mr Brent's families which we understood as a seal of approval, plus dozens of visitors from miles around.

The carol service was a stunning success and despite the flow of ale, this part of the evening was treated with due reverence much to the vicar's relief.

When the carols were over, the vicar thanked everyone for their participation and discreetly slipped out of the pub.

At this point, the singing changed to a more traditional and a somewhat more bawdy nature, helped no doubt by the Christmas spirit which was bought in prodigious quantities.

A great deal of money was collected for the 'Save The Children Fund' and everybody had a high old time witnessed by the fact that when we eventually closed, the charity collecting boxes had been forgotten and left behind in our tender care. They were claimed by their red faced guardians the following morning.

Most of the people who attended that night, returned over the Christmas period with friends and relatives and many became regular patrons from then on. That first Christmas really was the turning point in the fortunes of the Dog and Partridge. The success of the Carol evening at Mearsby, which incidentally, became a tradition, confirmed our feelings that provided we could arrange different events on a regular basis, then people would continue to enjoy their visits.

As it turned out, the sillier the events were, the more successful they became and many people came to our pub regularly in case they missed something.

One group of regulars confided that one of the reasons they came so often was because they never knew what would happen next.

Another reason was the quality of the beer.

Our beer was supplied by Ruddles, a small provincial brewery in Rutlandshire, whose product had several distinctive characteristics, not the least of which was strength.

Over the years, traditional draught beer served by gravity direct from the barrel behind the bar or hand pumped from the cellar had been gradually disappearing from pubs throughout the country.

It had been replaced largely with so called keg beers which from the breweries point of view were easier to store and transport amongst other things and from the publicans point of view were easier to keep and serve, needing little or no expertise to handle. In addition they were immediately ready to serve once connected to the beer line requiring no settling period after delivery to the pub.

From the beer drinkers viewpoint; well what did it matter? At the time, they had to buy what was available or at least that seemed to be the dictatorial attitude of many, but not all, of the larger breweries.

We were happy to be tied to Ruddles Brewery whose mission in life was to provide traditional beers to a discerning public. Even they however, were also producing keg variants of their distinctive beers.

Below the Bar

Traditional beer, or Real Ale, as it's known is made from pure water, malted barley and hop flowers to give the characteristic bitter flavour in addition to better keeping qualities. It's then fermented with yeast to convert the malt sugars into alcohol producing carbon dioxide in the process. Up to a certain point, the more sugar available for fermentation, the stronger the beer becomes. Beyond this point, the concentration of sugar actually kills the yeast cells which stops the fermentation process and results in a sweeter beer. Hops do not add to the alcoholic strength of the beer; only the flavour.

At the end of the initial fermentation, finings are added to the brew. These finings are often isinglass, a substance obtained from the swim bladder of the sturgeon. The finings ensure that the solid material such as worked out yeast cells fall to the bottom of the container in which the beer is kept.

The beer is pumped into a wooden cask which has two bungs so placed that a tap may be inserted into the end and that a peg may be used to pierce the top of the cask and provide a vent so that the carbon dioxide may be released as the beer finishes fermentation whilst reaching peak condition in the cask.

The cask is delivered to the Landlord before the beer is ready for drinking. It's his responsibility to ensure that the beer is kept cool. 55-58 degrees Fahrenheit being the optimum temperature and obviously a proper cellar is the ideal place for conditioning and storage.

The cask is placed on a raised platform, known as a thrall,

to prevent movement once it has been left to settle. The vent or spile bung is uppermost and the bung for tapping the barrel should be readily accessible at the front of the cask. With the barrel firmly chocked on the thrall, the first job is to drive a peg into the spile with a mallet. This vents the cask allowing the carbon dioxide to escape. The vent is then plugged with a soft or porous peg which allows the release of the gas but prevents any foreign bodies from entering the cask.

Once the barrel has been vented, the tap is driven into it with a sharp blow from the mallet which forces the tap bung straight into the cask. With practice it's possible to vent and tap a barrel without losing a drop of beer.

In my case, it took a lot of practice and in the early days many a gallon of Ruddles fine ales were lost.

In the interests of hygiene, it's important to ensure that all cellar equipment and indeed the bungs which are forced into the cask are scrupulously clean.

The beer now has to be left to settle and mature. My own experience showed that at least three days and very often a lot longer than that were necessary before the beer had reached peak condition. In an emergency, there was a trick which Enoch demonstrated, but which involved the loss of several gallons of beer, which would speed up the settling process so that it was more or less drinkable after 36 hours. This involved venting and tapping then immediately drawing off three or four gallons to encourage the downward movement of the solid matter in the cask.

The solid matter, through gravity and the action of the finings forms a sediment in the belly of the cask at a point below the level of the tap and provided due care is taken in tilting the barrel when the beer level falls, there is no reason why beer drawn from a cask should not be crystal clear.

The beer is drawn from the cask by a pipe connecting the barrel tap to a beer engine or more simply a suction pump operated either by hand or electricity. Before beer can be pulled, the spile peg has to be removed to allow air into the cask to replace the beer being drawn off, so it's clearly of paramount importance that the air in the cellar is as fresh and clean as humanly possible.

Notwithstanding the evil vinegar fly, a good landlord or cellarman knows that nothing spoils otherwise excellent beer more rapidly than foul or tainted air in the cellar.

He will therefore ensure that the floor, walls and ceiling are kept spotless, no stale beer or empty casks are allowed to remain in the cellar, ventilation channels or shafts are kept clear and no smoking is allowed in this very important area. When the bar is closed, the taps on the casks should be shut off and hard or solid pegs pushed into the spile to effectively seal the cask.

All beer lines and engines must be kept in a clean and spotless condition which involves a considerable amount of work but a clear, sparkling, full flavoured pint of beer served time after time does wonders for a pub's reputation.

Keg or bright beer is brewed in much the same way as traditional beer but extracts of hops and malt are often used in place of malt grains and hop flowers. When the fermentation is complete, the beer is filtered to remove all solid matter and then pasteurised producing a lifeless liquid reminiscent of cold tea. It's resurrected by the introduction of carbon dioxide pumped into kegs or containers with the beer under pressure. Under this pressure, the carbon dioxide remains in solution.

The beer is drawn from the keg by releasing a valve which allows the beer to escape whilst the pressure in the container is maintained by a connection to a carbon dioxide cylinder.

From a hygiene point of view, there is perhaps an advantage. The first contact the beer has with the outside air is when it leaves the bar dispenser.

In your glass, free from pressure, the carbon dioxide reverts to a gaseous state and gives the head and so called life to your otherwise pure but dead beer.

You will see from this the reasons why many breweries and publicans were not too enthusiastic about providing what is now popularly known as Real Ale!

To be fair to the publicans, the vast majority were unable to obtain traditional cask conditioned beer due to a reluctance, for whatever reasons, on the part of the breweries to which they were tied.

You would most likely have had a very interesting answer from your local publican had you asked him for his point of view on the subject.

At this point, mention must be made of CAMRA — The Campaign for Real Ale. These are a dedicated band of stalwarts who, in their early days, were treated as a bunch of hairy, noisy upstarts with a rather quaint desire to turn back the clock in their search for decent beer. In point of fact, they were underestimated in their determination to bring to the notice of beer lovers and other interested parties, the facts about traditional beers and the big business inspired near extinction of a great British heritage. Thanks to them and thousands of others who were not members of the organisation, Real Ale was demanded by the public at large and has grown in popularity as the years have gone by.

Next time you enjoy a pint of traditional ale, raise your glass to CAMRA. Without them it's likely that Real Ale would've been quietly done to death.

How did this affect the dear old Dog and Partridge?

For many years before our arrival on the scene, the only beer available there was served by gas pressure, our old friend carbon dioxide, in spite of the fact that one of the country's finest Real Ales was being produced by Ruddles.

The Reason?

The pub didn't have a proper cellar. This of course wasn't strictly true. It did have a cellar but it had been sealed up many years previously by a misguided brewery which by the time we took over the pub had long ceased to exist.

Above all, we wanted to sell cask conditioned beer and our customers wanted to buy it so we set about locating and opening our cellar.

Ruddles were very keen for us to sell Real Ale but not having detailed plans for the pub, were unable to help us with information on the whereabouts of the cellar. On the other hand, Enoch, Wilf and George were more than helpful.

Each of them was convinced where the cellar lay and each of them suggested a different site. Other villagers gave even more conflicting advice especially related to the site of the original delivery chute.

The arguments raged that it lay underneath the kitchen or beneath the bar. The delivery chute was either under a concrete screed which had been laid in the car park or according to Enoch was under the pavement at the front of the pub with another entrance at the rear under what by this time was a rose bed. As it turned out, Enoch's memory was the soundest but we had no way of knowing that at the time.

My brother Charles, who had come to live with us and help with the daily work, offered to dig a series of trenches to locate the buried entrances. The trenches grew in both length and depth until the place looked as though it was being fortified with a moat against some invader.

The villagers encouraged him in his labours, directed and then redirected him but nothing was found, much to their amusement. They were convinced by this time that we were all quite mad and I think that they may have had a point.

Then the brainwave struck! We had been tackling the job from the wrong end and I still do not know why we didn't think of it earlier. It could have been something to do with too much Ruddles County Ale.

Floorboards in the lounge were lifted and the first attempt revealed the cavern below. Our excitement at this discovery was made worse by Enoch leaping around the room shouting: 'By the left. Ah knew it... Ah bloddy knew it... Ah bloddy told yers. Oh you beauty. By the left.' The only way to calm him down was to give him a drink.

All we then had to do was find the original entrance.

It was dark, cold and dusty down there. The domain of overgrown spiders who had grown fat on the unwary insects who had made a one way visit.

The floor appeared to be crumbling concrete and the walls, lined with stone blocks whose lime-washed surfaces flaked and disintegrated at the slightest touch, had seen much better days.

But where was the exit or the entrance I suppose you would've called it once you were in the cellar. We rigged up an electric lamp and explored.

There, behind a mountain of rubble was a well worn stone staircase of 13 steps leading up to a ceiling of reinforced concrete. Calculations showed that ceiling to be the floor of our existing back room cellar where we kept the keg beer.

Provided we could break through from the top and make a large enough hole without seriously weakening the floor structure, then we were going to have an operational cellar.

Charles, who was a good man with a pick, hammer and bolster, set to with a will and smashed his way through nine inches of concrete reinforced with steel rods and coarse steel mesh. It took him two full days to make the hole and face up the edges with bricks and cement to complete a professional job. After that, the real work began.

Where it came from, we'll never know, but that cellar was full with something in excess of 25 tons of rubble. The floor wasn't, as we had first thought, a crumbling expanse of concrete but an ancient cobble stoned surface covered in lumps of brick, stone and dust. Huge blocks of masonry lay in heaps and the whole lot had to be cleared by hand. Bucketful by bucketful we hauled it up the steps and out to the rear car park.

Over the next few weeks, we scraped the walls and painted them along with the ceiling which we had to line to stop dust from falling from the lounge floor above. Ventilation shafts were cleared of old sacks, paper and spiders to produce a cellar of which we could be proud. It was large, cool, clean and functional.

Monty and Barney were pressed into service 'below stairs' for a week to ensure that any mice inhabiting the place were totally eradicated.

Ruddles supplied us with our first beer engine, a beautiful piece of engineering in brass with a porcelain handle, necessary cellar equipment and within a few weeks our first delivery of cask conditioned Ruddles County strong Ale was consigned to the cellar to settle and mature before serving.

Great Groats! Blessed Beer!

The arrival of Real Ale at the Dog and Partridge couldn't go unmarked so we arranged a centuries old custom of 'blessing the beer'. This was a rather doubtful medieval rite which was supposed to guarantee the quality of the ale for all time and generate feelings of well being in all those who imbibed. Ruddles County had that effect on most people after the first pint regardless of any properties allegedly bestowed upon it by magical rites!

I had spoken to a doctor friend, a member of the Dionysian Society, about the ceremony and as he was experienced in this sort of thing, he had agreed to dress in long white robes and officiate at the blessing. He gave me an outline of the form that the ceremony would take and it seemed to be just the sort of nonsense that would appeal to our regulars. In addition to his services, we had been promised another spectacular by the self styled members of the 'Wellington Club'. We were to know nothing about their own particular contribution until the day, however, they did say that they'd be accompanied by a band of wandering minstrels.

The local press was informed and the word went around our regulars and the local area by bush telegraph. Of special interest no doubt was the fact that we were giving away the first 18 gallons to be consumed at the ceremonials.

The great day dawned, and treated us kindly with a clear sky and warm early Spring sunshine.

On the stroke of midday we opened and the invasion began, slowly at first, until the whole pub, car park and gardens were packed with people obviously all out to enjoy themselves.

We had never seen so many people at the Dog and Partridge and long before everybody had got their first pint of Real Ale, the kilderkin we were giving away was empty. Fortunately, we had stocked up for an army and it looked as though we were going to need every drop.

I looked at the clock, 12.15pm and there was no sign of our white robed friend. The ceremony was due to begin at 12.30pm and we began to worry. 12.25pm came and there was still no sign of him and I could get no reply from his telephone.

There was nothing for it but to perform the rites myself...

PANIC!!!

I didn't even know the magical words but then thankfully nor did any of the people who had come along to watch.

Fortified by two very quick pints of County, equipped with a bucket, rope, giant wooden spoon, mallet and another pint of beer, I led a procession down to the bridge over the stream which ran not far from the pub and which was to be the site for the ceremony.

Surrounded by about 150 smiling faces, I tied the rope to the bucket and producing a banshee like scream which was supposed to sound more like a call to prayer, I lowered the bucket into the water then raised it to the parapet whilst chanting some seemingly appropriate words which I can't now remember. Following my scream, the crowd had fallen silent and then to my surprise and everlasting relief, they picked up the chant and kept it going.

I dipped my right elbow into the bucket of cool if somewhat brackish stream water and then dipped my left elbow into the pint of beer, hollered for silence and solemnly declared: 'Oh ale to be blessed. Thou art at one with the sweet coolness of the running stream. May thy flow forever be as pure.'

Then followed the blessing.

With the mallet and spoon raised above my head I chanted: 'Oh ale thou art once blessed' struck the spoon and mallet together then cast a 'groat' upon the stream. Groats were not available so I used a couple of tu'penny pieces.

This was repeated five times, each blessing greeted by a roar of approval from the crowd, many of whom thought that they had seen the faithful re-enactment of a centuries old custom and I wasn't going to be the one to tell them otherwise.

Back at the pub, with the beer flowing a lot faster than the stream which we had just left, another ceremony was just beginning.

The members of the 'Wellington Club', the significance of whose title I was now beginning to appreciate were on their knees in a circle, supping beer from a well worn Wellington boot accompanied by a jig played on a violin and a penny whistle.

The first person to draw breath without emptying the boot had to pay for the refill and took no further part in the bout. This continued until only one person was left and he naturally enough was presented with the boot and entitled 'Keeper of the Welly'.

I couldn't help thinking about all the preparation that went into serving the beer in pristine condition and all they could do was drink it out of a dirty old Wellington boot. It was a hilarious ceremony, enjoyed more by those who watched than those who took part, I suspect, but nonetheless added to the general air of lunacy surrounding our introduction of Real Ale.

The upshot of all this activity was an increase in the numbers of people visiting our little pub and a reputation for unusual activities in which you would be very welcome to join or merely to watch and laugh along with it.

The day after the ceremony, people I hadn't seen before were stopping me in the main street of Rushford and talking about the previous day's happenings. I was puzzled at first that news had spread so quickly until I picked up my copy of the daily county newspaper.

Imagine my feelings when I saw that my sense of the ridiculous was being publicised all over the County. There on the front page was a photograph of a lunatic sitting astride a bridge parapet waving a spoon and mallet to the amusement of those around him.

The description of the event was even more horrifying. It had been described as, 'a serious and ancient custom. A medieval rite'.

Well perhaps it will become one in due time.

The Domino Factor

Although darts were no longer played at our pub for reasons already explained, we were the home of a thriving dominoes team of which George, Enoch and his wife Edna were proud and able members.

The game played in the local league was called 'fives and threes' for reasons which we'll come to and each team consisted of eight members who would be drawn by lot, organised by the team captains, into pairs who would play together against a pair from the opposing team. Thus each table would have four players and there would be four tables in play during a league match.

Enoch had made it quite clear that he wouldn't play if Edna was drawn as his partner and although he never explained why, I suspect it was because when the game developed, a player could pass on the blame to his partner for any mistakes made, a trick at which Enoch was particularly adept, and Edna was the only one who wouldn't leave the resulting argument behind when they left the pub.

Whatever the reason was, it never ceased to amaze me that they were never drawn to play together. We all suspected collusion between the captain and Enoch but if that was the case, they were very clever and secretive about it.

The very first home match we experienced caused us problems. For a start we didn't know where to set up the special tile topped tables with their matching chairs and then of course there were the personalities.

Shortly before our arrival at the Dog and Partridge, Wilf, a domino player since boyhood, had been dropped from the team because he had been unable to see the spots very well and had been making error after error, not only with the run of play but also with his scoring which was kept with pins in a holed, brass faced tablet of wood, rather like a cribbage board.

His mistakes were understood by his team mates but not necessarily by the opposition who would often be upset by his apparent negligence.

Poor old Wilf was still smarting from what he considered to be the insult of not being selected to play and he clearly intended to make a nuisance of himself. Having taken his mild and bitter from the bar, he marched, stick in hand straight to one of the prepared match tables, took a seat and glared defiantly at everyone around him.

The match was ready to start but Wilf refused to move despite pleading from me, followed by Jane, the two team captains and all the players who were by now becoming rather impatient with the cantankerous old rogue.

'Oi've sat in this 'ere chair far longer n'yous lot 've even used t' pub n'oim not bloody moving fer any o'yers.'

Like a flash, the thought struck me. I had just repaired a chair that was obviously a lot older than anything else in the pub, including Wilf. I rushed upstairs to get it and returned to see 16 angry faces surrounding the seemingly implacable Wilf.

I put the chair down in front of him and lied. 'This is your chair Wilf. At least that's what Charlie the last landlord told me. I've repaired it for you.'

Well, whether I had just struck lucky and had in fact stumbled across Wilf's old chair or he just liked the look of it, I'll never know, but he examined it closely, then carried it almost lovingly to the other side of the fireplace.

'Alright yous lot. Gerron wi' yers game,' he grumbled. 'But remember this 'ere is my chair 'n no-one else is gonna use 'n.'

From that moment on it was Wilf's personal chair and those in the know never used it when he was about. Any strangers occupying his seat when he came in were soon made aware of their mistake. They'd look up to see an angry old man with a quivering walrus moustache hovering next to them and glaring into their eyes. Without a word being said, they'd always move and Wilf would resume his rightful place.

If you have never seen a domino match, particularly 'fives and threes', in progress, I suggest you find a pub where they play the game and go along to watch just for the experience. It defies adequate description but I will try.

Players go in turn and the 'card' they place on the table has to match at one end, the 'card' which is already there so if the line of dominoes on the table has, for instance, a six at one end and a two at the other, then the next player has to possess a six or a two 'card' in order to play his turn. Score is achieved by adding the values of the two ends of the line and if the total is divisible by three or five then the number of times it can be divided by those numbers is the point or points scored. e.g. At one end of the line is a double six and at the other is a three, then the total is 15. 15 divided by 3 gives 5. The total points scored therefore are eight. The two partners combine their scores and the first pair to complete two circuits of the scoreboard win the game. Simple isn't it!

Each table plays three games and the match is decided on the number of games won or lost rather than on table wins so it's possible for a team to win on two tables, lose on two tables and yet still win the match; a situation which, without fail, raises the feelings of the losing side.

The sight of 16 grown men and women as excited over the progress of their game as schoolchildren in a playground, the silence whilst play was underway and the swell of sound as the dominoes were shuffled, reaching a crescendo with howls of anguish at losing and cries of delight from the victors, always made us laugh, particularly that first night when we had never seen anything like it.

In addition to the playing members of the team, each side would have at least one 'runner' whose job it was to ensure that his or her team mates never ran out of drink thereby ensuring that the game never interfered with the real reason for being at the pub. As a reward, every time a runner took drinks to a table, he would receive a free refill from whoever was buying the round so you can imagine that there was rarely a shortage of volunteers for that coveted position.

These evenings would end with a raffle, from the proceeds of which we'd, by tradition, take the costs of preparing sandwiches for each table. As well as the usual prizes of bottles of beer, cigarettes and cigars, we made a point of having a couple of booby prizes to raise a laugh or two. These could be anything from a box of matches to a stick of licquorice but one was particularly memorable.

During one domino season (oh yes... they even have a season for the game) there was an acute shortage of potatoes and we had put on the prize tray amongst flagons of cider, boxes of cigars and packs of cigarettes, one enormous spud.

Mrs Jenkins, the team captain's mother had won first pick from the tray and to a roar of laughter from everyone promptly chose the potato.

'It's no wha' it's worth m' dears,' she explained. 'It's whether yous can get the darn things. An' oi can't.'

Following another match, George swayed up to the bar to return the dominoes and the scoreboard saying: 'Oi prefers our normal scoreboard. this 'n's wooden an' yers can't see the 'oles in 'n too well. Le' us 'ave t' brass 'n next toim'.

'Aye. Daft Bugger!' said Enoch turning the board over. 'Yous 'ad t'bloddy thing upside down all night.'

Following the demise of the darts team which happened within a couple of weeks of our arrival at the pub, the domino players were naturally concerned about the future of their own game as representatives of the Dog and Partridge.

In order to reassure them, I decided to try and master the intricacies of 'fives and threes' and to play the odd game with the locals whenever possible. Once you have watched the others and played a few times, the actual game seems reasonably easy and you can become a fairly average player in quite a short time. The real skill comes with practice and the ability to interpret your partner's strengths and weaknesses and to recognise your opponents' bluff when it happens.

The other skill is purely one of physical co-ordination and requires a player to hold seven ivory 'cards' in his hand so that only he can see them whilst keeping at least two fingers and a thumb of the other hand free to place the appropriate 'card' on the table. If you have never done it before, try it.

It's not easy.

Eventually, in recognition of my willingness to support the team, Bernard, the captain, asked me to play in a match against one of the weaker league teams.

I was partnered with Paul, a 20 stone amiable giant, who took his dominoes very seriously but always tried to appear nonchalant about the game. That night, unknown to either of us, his patience was to be severely tried ...so we sat down to play.

The first game was uneventful. Paul had offered to follow my lead and to play to whatever I laid on the table. Unknown to me, I should've laid the 'cards' in a certain order which would've indicated to Paul, the relative merits of my hand. We won the game more, I'm sure, by luck than judgement and by confusing our opponents who no doubt were looking for signs of what my hand contained and playing accordingly.

The second game was different. With growing confidence, I picked up the 'cards' I had been dealt and attempted to hold them close to my chest. One ivory slipped and before I knew it, the other six cards' had fallen face up onto the table.

'Bloody 'ell,' exploded Paul. 'We'll 'ave ter bloody reshuffle 'n look wha' ad in me 'and.'

Combined with the 'cards' that I had dropped, Paul had held a domino player's dream. Played properly, we could have taken an unassailable lead. The replacement hand dealt to us was hopeless and we went on to lose the second game by a big margin.

'Sorry Paul,' I muttered. 'My fault entirely. But we're all square with one to go.'

Paul tried to smile but underneath he was very upset. I bought everyone a drink.

The third and final game began and we took an early lead. As luck would have it, the play went in our favour, then, seeing an opportunity to take the maximum eight points, I excitedly leaned over the table with the necessary 'card' and promptly knocked over two pints of beer. One over me and the other over Paul. Our opponents escaped the drenching.

'Bloody 'ell,' said Paul with feeling. 'He's bloody well at it agin. Le's get this bloody game over wi'.'

Paul's turn came and he took the points to win the game and the match. 'Thank God for that,' I thought. 'He'd never have forgiven me if we had lost.'

All was forgiven however, but I was only invited to play on one other occasion and that was an emergency, when, because of sickness, we couldn't raise a full team. Under the league rules, that would've meant forfeiting three games in the match total and I suppose Bernard took the view that I couldn't do any worse than that. As it turned out, playing with the wily Enoch, we won all three games. It has to be recorded though, that at the end of season celebration, I was the only one with a 100 percent record of winning.

Things That Go Bump in the Night

Every old country pub should have one. If it hasn't, then invent one. That's what publicans up and down the country were doing to attract tourists and boost trade.

We didn't invent one... it was invented for us by my mother or rather I should say, they were both invented by her.

...I'm talking about ghosts!

If you're imaginative and a little nervous, then living in an old and remote house is the ideal way to see and hear ghostly figures.

Mother stayed with us for about three weeks so that she could decorate the upper part of the house, putting it in a good enough condition for us to let the rooms to paying guests.

At the very top of the house, in the garret, it was dark and lonely. The wind whistled around the dormer windows and moaned softly in the telegraph wires as the timbers groaned and creaked under the weight of the Collyweston tiled roof.

At night, these sounds seemed louder and less friendly than in the daytime whilst the yellow light from an old butane lamp cast an eerie glow and made the shadows dance around the room. Occasionally, an owl could be heard hooting to its mate. Foxes would be heard coughing and sighing on the edge of Mearsby Copse. All these sounds would mingle chillingly in the damp stillness of the room. Mother was convinced that the Dog and Partridge was haunted and the garret was most likely the place where it would manifest itself.

Given her fears, why she insisted in decorating the garret at night, I shall never know but one evening, she insisted on working alone whilst Jane and I managed the bar.

After a couple of hours, I decided to see how she was getting on with her work and climbed the two flights of stairs which led to the garret.

I found her sitting on the dark oak staircase, wide eyed, pale and visibly shaken with her head tilted to one side and straining to hear something.

She was terrified, although she never admits to it, and raised a shaking hand to silence me as I approached her. 'Shh... be quiet. Can't you hear it?' The words cracked out of her parched throat.

'Hear what Mum?' I asked cheerfully but feeling the tension in the air.

'Be quiet. You'll hear it. There it is again. Now!' She cried with her eyes nearly popping out of her head.

And there it was. An awful sound. Awful that's when you're sitting all alone on a spooky staircase in semi darkness and expecting a supernatural visitation at any time.

CRASH! SCRAPE! SCRABBLE! followed by an ever increasing growling noise that sounded like demons from Hell working their way through the very fabric of the house.

I grinned and led her down the stairs to our sitting room situated directly above the bar.

'You'll hear it again in here Mum, but I think you'll find it will sound a little different as we're that much closer,' I explained.

CRASH! went the dominoes as they were struck face down on the tile topped tables. SCRAPE... SCRABBLE... they went as they were shuffled and redistributed. A swell of growling sounds were heard as the locals argued the toss about the outcome of the previous game.

Mother, by this time, fully composed, smiled weakly at me. 'I see what you mean,' then promptly added in a voice full of authority: 'I still think this place is haunted.'

We didn't realise just how jumpy she was about the wretched 'ghost' until just before she went to bed that night when she expressed her concern for her dog whom she had brought with her. He was a huge, fearless but good natured German Shepherd called Kaiser who she felt was being disturbed by the 'presence' and would be much better off if he slept in her room, next to her bed. She explained at some length that this proposed arrangement wasn't for her benefit but simply in the interests of Kaiser's continued well being.

A few days later, she confronted me with firm evidence that her bedroom was being shared with a ghost. No! She hadn't actually seen it but Kaiser had heard or sensed it and had spent the previous nights padding restlessly in the room. I pointed out that he wasn't used to sleeping in a bedroom and would probably take some time to adjust to his new surroundings.

'Then how d'you explain this?' she asked, producing a white sweater with what appeared to be bloodstains spattered over it. 'That's blood and neither Kaiser nor I have cut ourselves. You can't explain that away. It's proof positive... I tell you that this room is definitely haunted and I'm moving into another.'

In the bar, she spread the story to anybody who was willing to listen and before long, it was a well known fact that the Dog and Partridge, like so many other old pubs, was definitely haunted.

The stains on the sweater really had me puzzled for a long time and I was unable to find a rational explanation until we had a visit from Jane's parents.

We put them in the 'haunted' room and sure enough, reddy brown stains appeared on a white shirt.

Laurence, Jane's father said: 'I put it on that stool last night, fresh, clean and ready for this morning. I don't know how it happened.'

That's when we found out. Above the stool was an old oak beam and out of the cracks would occasionally fall a few specks of reddy brown powder. The after effects of wood worm attacks during 400 years of service. Any dampness in the air or on the clothes concerned would immediately be absorbed by the powder to produce the 'bloodstains'.

I telephoned my mother to explain the mystery but she refused to be convinced saying: 'All that's as maybe but you needn't expect me to stay in that room again.'

On subsequent visits she never did. Despite the trauma of ghosts and ghoulies, mother had done a superb job renovating the personal living quarters and bedrooms of the house so that within a short time we were able to offer bed and breakfast accommodation in simple but clean and pleasant surroundings at the princely sum of two pounds per person per night.

Wakey Wakey... Rise and Shine!

Our entry into the bed and breakfast business brought a new dimension to our efforts at inn-keeping and with it a whole new crop of experiences.

Whilst the vast majority of our guests were quite normal people who would come and go without incident, there were of course those whose stay at the Dog and Partridge will never be forgotten. At least not by Jane and I.

Because of the rigours of keeping a bar, we were rarely in bed before 1.00am. This made it difficult to guarantee our guests an early morning call with the usual tea or coffee in bed so we supplied an alarm clock in each room so that people could make their own arrangements. We'd discuss, before they went to bed, their requirements for breakfast and at what time the meal would be needed the following morning.

This arrangement worked extremely well until David and Joan arrived for a week's lodgings.

They were both 20 years old or thereabouts and hadn't been married very long. I suspected that David wasn't very sure of himself and that his aggressive, complaining nature was just a symptom of his self-consciousness. It manifested itself in his seemingly total inability to say please or thank you and his attitude that Jane and I had been hired along with his room as his personal servants.

'When will you be ready for breakfast?' I asked on his first night. 'Eight o'clock sharp,' he snapped. I resolved to make allowances for his brusque behaviour.

At 7.15 the following morning, I tapped on his door to

make sure that they didn't oversleep. 'Alright Alright, I know what time it is,' came the rude reply.

We laid a table for them in the breakfast room. Three types of cereal, two racks of toast, butter, jam, marmalade and pots of tea and coffee completed the scene. At eight o'clock they arrived and wishing them a good morning, I asked them to help themselves to the cereal whilst I cooked their eggs and bacon. In reply, I received a slight smile from Joan and a grunt from David.

Five minutes later, the kitchen door burst open.

'Where the hell's my eggs and bacon,' he demanded. 'I told you eight o'clock and it's now five past. I'm not interested in that other stuff on the table. You told me my breakfast would be ready at eight and by breakfast I mean the fried stuff. Now hurry it up!'

I had a mental picture of this arrogant young man framed in the doorway with fried eggs, bacon and tomatoes slithering down his face but resisted the temptation to make it happen. My anger was rising but I bit my lip and suggested that he rejoined his wife and that I would serve their breakfast directly. Inwardly fuming, I completed the cooking and at eight minutes past eight served up two plates of still sizzling eggs, bacon, tomatoes, sausage and fried bread. Joan murmured her thanks and he snapped: 'About time too!'

He came closer to wearing his breakfast at that moment than he will ever realise. 10 minutes later, they were moving around and obviously ready to leave. Joan had eaten her plateful and quietly said: 'Thanks. That was delicious.' Not so his Lordship. 'Too damn hot to eat,' he growled and off they went.

I vented my fury on a pile of logs that needed splitting. I had made enough allowances for this young man's bad manners and churlish behaviour and resolved to teach him a lesson.

That night, after dinner, they sat in the bar and drank steadily. When I sensed that they were about to retire for the night, I said, bubbling over with goodwill and friendliness, 'Don't go up yet. Have a drink with us. On the house.' Pouring them both large scotches, I managed to get them talking. Joan talked about the local countryside and David, not surprisingly, about himself.

The whiskies bought first by us and then by them were doing their job and when our guests were quite drunk and burbling merrily, I said: 'Well folks, time's getting on. We mustn't be late in the morning.' With cheery goodnights all round, we helped them stumble up the stairs to their room.

At 7.15am the following day, I tip-toed past their room and by the snoring sounds which I heard, was convinced that they were fast asleep. Excellent, I thought malevolently as I arrived at the kitchen to prepare breakfast. Having cooked and served their meal, I waited until the stroke of eight, when I raced up the stairs and hammered on their door. 'Wakey wakey... Rise and shine,' I bellowed. 'It's eight o'clock and breakfast is on the table. Come on. Shake a leg. You don't want to be late do you?!'

Smiling with malicious pleasure, I sneaked off to the kitchen and waited.

10 minutes later, two harassed, hung over and pathetic looking people sat at the table, avoiding their cold fried

breakfast but drinking the strong black coffee that we had provided.

David's red rimmed and sore looking eyes gazed at me as he said so very politely: 'Do you have an aspirin or an Alka Seltzer PLEASE?'

That evening David met me in the passage upstairs. 'Nick,' he said. 'I'd like to apologise for what you've had to put up with. Can we call a truce please?'

'Truce,' I replied. 'We're not at war are we?' Laughing I suggested that we had a drink to show that there were no hard feelings. 'Er... No thanks,' he replied, no doubt still feeling the effects of the previous night's session. 'I... er... don't think I'd better. Perhaps tomorrow night eh?'

After that they were both excellent guests and I am sure that they enjoyed the rest of their stay as much as we did.

On the other side of the coin were some of the most helpful and willing guests whose cooperation seemingly knew no bounds. One young man by the name of Geoff, who stayed with us for about six weeks, was known privately by us as the ideal guest.

After breakfast on the first morning he said: 'Your farmhouse breakfast was superb but please from now on, half that amount will be plenty for me.' His breakfast dishes were neatly stacked on the edge of the table and by the time I had taken them to the kitchen and returned, he had removed the table cloth, folded it and left it on the sideboard. He went to work and Jane went to his room to dust round and make his bed. She returned a few minutes later with a big smile on her face. 'He's made his own bed and there's not a thing out of place,' she said.

In the evenings, he would often be found in the wash up behind the bar, busily polishing glasses or attending to some odd job that needed doing. All things considered it was almost, but not quite, an embarrassment to take his money at the end of each week such was his assistance in the smooth running of the pub.

I do not mind admitting that when he left to move into his new home, we really missed the help that he had given us.

Another guest who was accepted by my brother Charles in our absence one evening was a long distance lorry driver called Bob. Charles had told us that Bob had booked a single room for Tuesday and Thursday nights for the following four weeks. 'Fine,' I said. 'But d'you realise what time lorry drivers like to get up?'

'Ah,' replied Charles. 'I hadn't thought about that but don't worry. I'll give him a call and cook his breakfast if he wants it early.'

Bob duly arrived and as expected liked to be on the road by 6.30 in the morning. Charles groaned in despair.

'Don't worry about breakfast,' said Bob. 'I would prefer to take some sandwiches with me and you could make those tonight.' Charles brightened a little. 'But I would like some coffee at about six if that's possible please.'

Charles groaned again, but, good as his word, he agreed to make the early morning drink. In the event, he only had to do it once. On subsequent visits, Bob would rise early, make his own coffee and take a cup into Charles who would then get up and unlock the pub so that Bob could get on his way. It was a system that, worked well for both of them.

Probably our most memorable guest was Cliff who stayed for one night only. Small in stature, he had a high pitched voice which made itself heard all over the pub. He had a permanent smile on his face which glowed like a beacon after one pint of County ale giving it a comical expression which tended to attract the attention of anybody looking for a butt for their jokes.

To make matters worse for him, he encouraged the attention by taking a very real interest in what he overheard or was being told. 'People always take the mickey out of me,' he slurred as he reached uncertainly for his fourth pint. 'But I don't mind. It makes them happy. I love them all.' 'Too bloody right,' whispered Charles who suspected that Cliff was taking more than a passing interest in him. He needn't have worried. A few minutes later he said to Jane as she pulled him a pint. 'I'd rather you served my beer. You're much better looking than Charles.'

He then set about the time honoured tradition of chatting up the barmaid, blissfully unaware that the attractive young blonde he was clumsily and comically trying to impress, was in fact the landlady.

Having made no progress, he turned his attention to two of our regulars, Conor and Anne who were sitting by the inglenook. 'Barmaid's a nice girl,' he shrilled. 'But I haven't seen the landlady yet. What's she like?'

Instantly recognising a joke in the making, Conor advised: 'A dragon. She breathes fire and God help you if you don't behave yourself. Oh yes! and you'd do well to keep away from young Jane or the Dragon will skin you alive.'

'Blimey! she sounds a right tyrant,' he gulped.

Unaware as to the reasons why, we noticed Cliff studiously avoiding Jane and insisting that his drinks were served by Charles whose earlier suspicions were once again aroused.

'I don't know about you Nick,' he confided. 'But my door will be firmly locked tonight. I'm just not sure about that Cliff.'

Some time later, when the bar had been closed and the four of us were enjoying a nightcap, I noticed Cliff nervously glancing over his shoulder every few moments.

'What's the trouble Cliff? I asked. 'You seem uneasy.'

'He's not the only one,' whispered Charles.

'Well,' said Cliff. 'I don't know how the landlady is related to any of you but from what I've heard, she sounds a bit dangerous and I've not met her yet.'

'Then let me introduce you Cliff,' I smirked. 'This is Jane Roberts, my wife and landlady of the Dog and Partridge at Mearsby.'

'Oh my God. They've been pulling my leg again. Oh God and I thought... Blimey and I've been chatting you up... Oh God I'm sorry, I didn't realise.'

We couldn't stop laughing but fortunately, through years of experience no doubt, Cliff didn't stay embarrassed for long and laughed along with us.

The time came for bed and Cliff told us he wanted to be up

at 8.30. Quickly Charles piped up, 'I forgot to warn you about the guard dog Cliff and I strongly recommend that you don't leave your room until 8.30 when he will have been fed and chained up again.'

'Oh don't worry about me,' replied Cliff. 'I like dogs.'

'You won't like this one,' said Charles convincingly. 'He's a rare brute.'

'What sort is he?' asked Cliff a little nervously.

'Specially bred to be savage,' went on Charles. 'His father was a violent Doberman and his mother was the most evil tempered German Shepherd bitch I've ever had the misfortune to meet. Satan, that's his name by the way, has the worst traits from both his parents and his job here is to patrol the house at night. He ranges freely from top to bottom and if he caught anyone wandering about, he'd tear their throat out without a second thought. I'm telling you this for your own benefit Cliff, because we can't be responsible once we release the brute.'

Cliff was convinced, went straight to bed and bolted his door.

'What a load of twaddle.' I said to Charles.

'Maybe,' he replied. 'But at least it'll make sure he doesn't leave his room tonight.'

I had to laugh when I thought about Houdini, friend of the world and his wife, as a ferocious and terrifying guard dog.

Cliff had obviously believed every word because at 8.15 the following morning, he shouted from his room: 'Have you got that bloomin' dog out of the way yet?'

'No problem,' replied Charles. 'He's out in the yard.'

Cliff came down to his breakfast after which, he decided to

take a stroll in the garden. He opened the back door in time to see a white and orange streak leaping towards him. Slamming the door, he cried: 'Blimey, the brute nearly got me.'

'I think the time has come to tell the truth,' chortled Charles. 'Come and meet Houdini.'

Cliff and our daft Setter immediately made friends, with Houdini showing off his repertoire of leaping antics.

A half hour or so later, I overheard Cliff talking to the dog and felt quite ashamed. 'We're two of a kind Houdini, everybody takes the mickey out of us but we never bite back do we?'

A week after he'd stayed with us, Cliff wrote a letter saying how much he had enjoyed his visit and hoped to be able to stay again. Sadly, he never did.

Tact and Diplomacy

Diplomacy and tact should be among the attributes possessed by a publican and although I tried, I never seemed quite able to get the hang of it. There were of course those people with whom we could trade insults on a purely conversational basis and kept within limits, this friendly badinage offended nobody. There were a few occasions when the limits were exceeded but generally speaking, the most embarrassing incidents occurred accidentally during unguarded moments. There were also times when temperament gained the upper hand and I became downright objectionable to those who I considered were taking an unfair advantage of my otherwise fairly easy going nature.

Shortly after we had taken over the pub, we had made it known that nobody under the age of 18 would be allowed in the lounge and this change had been largely welcomed and respected by our customers.

One Sunday lunchtime, a smartly dressed young man stood at the bar accompanied by a dumpy, fresh faced lad wearing crumpled denim jeans and a sloppy tee shirt which, across the chest, sported the legend 'WhizzRocket' together with a print of some kind of spaceship.

The smart one was clearly in his 20s but I had serious doubts about his companion. Another look at the T-shirt convinced me; I had to let him know about the minimum age restriction especially as other people in the bar had gone along with it.

Leaning across the counter, I quietly spoke to the young

man. Unfortunately, two things happened at that precise moment. There was a lull in the general buzz of conversation and the record being played reached the end of its last track. Rather like the man on the tube train who finds himself shouting a private message to his wife as the clatter stops on arrival at a station, my voice echoed around the room,

'I'm sure you didn't realise, but we do not allow young lads in here any more but please feel free to use the snug bar if you wish.' I said nodding towards the tee shirt.

Polite but firm I thought.

The silence continued with shattering intensity; all eyes were on the young man as his smile faded into a twitching around the corners of his mouth.

'I beg your pardon,' he said in a slightly raised voice as though he hadn't quite caught what I had said.

It was by now even quieter in the bar and everybody had taken an interest in the proceedings.

Confidently I repeated what I had said.

His face contorted into a mask of fury as he glared at me with as much venom as he could muster. His head jerked convulsively as he bellowed at me: 'She, I repeat SHE, SHE, SHE isn't under 18, SHE is 22...'

Oh dear, I had clearly struck a blow at his ego and he wasn't going to let me off lightly. For once in my life, I was lost for words but the situation was saved for me at any rate by George who let out a huge guffaw and slid off his stool onto the carpet with laughter.

George had a very infectious laugh and before long, many others had joined him with the exception of the young man and his girlfriend who I must admit, never returned to our hostelry for another try.

Conor came in one evening with two friends, Ron and Sheila, whom we hadn't previously met. They were friendly enough and chatted with us quite merrily. They had been married for some years and lived in a narrow boat moored quite some distance away on the River Nene. As they didn't have a car, they were unable to visit us on a regular basis.

I always tried to remember names, faces and the odd scrap of conversation so that on subsequent occasions, visitors would feel welcome and remembered as individuals. The thought that stuck in my mind this time was that Sheila, a rather plain dark haired girl was pregnant.

Some months later, Ron came back alone to the pub and we nattered for a short while until I said: 'Has Sheila had her baby yet.'

'Baby?' he said. 'What baby? she's not pregnant, never has been. She may be fat but she's not pregnant.' ...CLANG!

Feeling the blood rushing to my face, I swiftly tried to wriggle out of it and unwittingly dug a deeper hole for myself. 'I could have sworn she said something about a baby,' I lied. 'I must be confusing her with someone else.'

'No you're not,' he pressed on relentlessly. 'I know she's fat, she knows she's fat and now you know she's fat so there's no need for you to try and cover up.'

Fortunately, Ron had a great sense of humour and having

made me want to crawl away into a dark corner, bought me a pint to, as he put it, 'cool down your cheeks before they burst into flame'.

Another classic conversational error occurred shortly after we had moved into the pub. We were being plagued by a noisy character, by the name of McAllister, an ex-landlord, whose pub had been sold by the brewery without him being offered an alternative house. We and the others who knew him drew our own conclusions. Despite our inexperience, we certainly didn't think that he was qualified to tell us how to run our newly acquired pub and asked him to keep his voice down and to keep his advice to himself. I secretly resolved to ban him at the first opportunity. The young man at the bar nodded sympathetically but took no real notice of McAllister's constant interruptions and continued to chat to me about everyday matters.

Something McAllister said, finally made me see red. Spitefully I said to him: 'You weren't capable of running your own pub so don't try to tell me how to run mine. Now finish your drink and go. Don't bother to come back in the future because you won't be served.'

I turned, still angry, to the young man at the bar and said: 'I'm trying to rid this place of loud mouthed, overbearing oafs like that.'

He finished his pint saying: 'I don't really blame you but don't expect to see me here again either.'

Turning his attention to a red faced McAllister he said: 'C'mon Dad. I'd better take you home,' as the pair of them left the bar for the last time.

A short time later, a lady at the bar asked me, 'Why don't you ask the Hunt to meet here when they're in the area.'

'Yes,' added her daughter. 'It's a colourful sight. It would be good publicity not to mention extra business.'

They had struck one of my pet hates and I replied hastily: 'The last thing I need in my pub is a crowd of bloodthirsty, hysterical, pink clad barbarians whose sole aim is to glorify in the name of sport, the murderous pursuit of a terrified and defenceless animal whose only crime is the taking of the odd pheasant which it needs for its very survival. No thank you and furthermore...'

I got no further. They slammed down their glasses and left.

'Boy you've certainly got a way wi' folks,' said Enoch as he came to the bar. 'S'good t' see yers stand up fer summat but d'yers know who they were.'

'No!' I replied. 'But I bet they like fox hunting.'

'Right boy, right first time an' I'll tell yers summat else. Yers jes added insult to injury. Thu's owd McAllister's missus and daughter.'

As you can imagine, we never had a 'meet' at the pub and not surprisingly, never again saw a McAllister.

The group of 10 strangers seemed ordinary enough when they came in one Saturday night. This was the night when Jane, assisted by a local girl called Irene, would serve upwards of 80 meals being mainly steaks or fish, between 7.30pm and 10.30pm.

We made a point of ensuring that the rump steak we bought was of good quality and would buy three or four whole rumps to cope with the expected weekend rush. I personally carved the meat into individual steaks and any that were too fatty or too skimpy, we reserved for personal consumption, thus making certain that to the best of our knowledge, the steaks we served would be enjoyable.

We operated the catering on a much lower than usual profit margin and I suspect that it was the combination of low cost and high quality which made our meal and snack trade such a success.

In spite of our efforts, it was obviously possible for a tough steak to be cooked and served and on the rare occasions when this happened, we'd gladly replace the meal. To safeguard ourselves and to let people know that we cared, we'd always check that our customers were satisfied with everything shortly after starting their meal.

We followed this procedure with the party of 10 and apart from sarcastic comments, which I ignored, about the lack of trimmings such as watercress and German mustard, they confirmed that their steaks were good and cooked to their liking.

Half an hour later, one of the group came to the bar and paid for the meals declaring so that everyone could hear.

'We like your pub and your Real Ale but your cooking's

bloody lousy.'

Remembering tact and diplomacy, I left the bar and walked with him to his table, inwardly seething because I knew the care we took with meals and that we certainly didn't deserve that kind of comment, especially with a pub full of people waiting for a steak. Significantly, one of the women who had made the sarcastic comments earlier piped up: 'Tough as old boots they were so we're taking the remains home for the dog if he can manage to eat them.' She then giggled to her friends.

If it had been her purpose to annoy me, she had succeeded but I didn't react with an angry outburst although it was never far from the surface. Instead, I thought I would treat them in kind. Many of our regulars were busily tucking into their food so one by one I asked them out loud for their comments and one by one I got them loud and clear.

'Delicious', 'Melts in your mouth', 'Excellent', 'Don't know how you do it for the price', 'Best you can buy round here', 'No complaints at all' and 'As good as ever'.

That was just the support I wanted and turned on the group who by now had stopped laughing and didn't appear to be so confident especially as I had already taken their money at the bar.

Now beginning to take a malicious pleasure in what I was about to do and knowing that I had the full attention of everybody in the pub I declared: 'You must have all been terribly unlucky. Let me see the remains of your steaks and I'll take them to the kitchen and see what my wife can do for you.'

The 'remains' were simply two or three small pieces of fat

without a trace of tough meat.

I took them to the kitchen where Jane, absolutely infuriated, when she learned what had happened, helped me with the next stage.

I returned to the bar with a plastic bag full of food scraps, a tin of dog meat and a handful of dog biscuits which I presented to the complaining woman who was clearly the ringleader. 'There Madam,' I said. 'With the compliments of the house. We wouldn't want your dog to starve. Now kindly leave while our regular customers are still reasonably friendly.'

Amid a chorus of boos and catcalls, they fled, never to return. Our regulars were really looking after us.

It was months later that we found out that the gang of 10 bad been 'planted' on us by the landlord of a nearby pub. Apparently we had decimated his food trade.

Two of our memorable customers were Gerald and Andrew who owned and ran the local hairdressing salon in Rushford.

They were business partners in addition to being partners in life and had a wonderfully steady relationship with each other and were quite open about being homosexuals which was quite remarkable in the mid-70s (I hate the cynical hijacking of the word 'gay' which in days gone by meant happy and carefree).

After we took over the Dog and Partridge, they came to see us and asked if they could visit us on a regular basis because they liked a night out but confessed that they were were made obviously and horribly unwelcome in most if not all of the the local hostelries because of their, at that time, peculiarly conceived sexual orientation.

As a landlord, you can't show any prejudice so I had a quiet chat with them explaining that they'd always be welcome at our house providing that they didn't try to 'hit' on any of our other male customers. That just shows how ignorant I was about the way these absolute gentlemen behaved.

They took my comments in good part with an understanding which must have been rooted in the general attitude inflicted upon them by the majority of people in those days.

As it turned out, they were model customers, always dressed very smartly, impeccably behaved and bitching at each other like any other married couple on a night out.

Our other regulars were ambivalent towards them and accepted their presence without snide comments apart from the odd nudge and wink when the beer started to flow.

To be honest, as far as we were concerned, Gerald and Andrew were probably the most polite and well behaved regular customers that we were privileged to have had.

One night, they approached us saying that they were hoping to have a visit from some of their special friends from London and wondered if we'd mind them having their little but clearly very important reunion celebration at our pub. My response, as ever, was that if they behaved themselves, as they always did, and that their friends behaved likewise, there would be no problem and that they'd all be welcome and treated as honoured guests at our little hostelry.

Their great night came and they minced into the pub with their special friends who were dressed in Savile Row suits, beautiful silk shirts complete with designer ties clipped into their shirts with solid gold clasps which must have cost a small fortune and with an air of confidence which could only have come from the recommendation which Gerald and Andrew had given them about the welcome which they were likely to receive. Their hair was magnificently cut and styled and their fingernails were manicured to perfection. They approached the bar and almost in unison said: 'It's so so nice to be able to come to a pub, even a little one like this, way out in the country here where we feel safe away from the city, and it's so so nice of you to accept us with our special friends Gerry and Andy.' 'Bless you, you little tinker,' said one of them. I was embarrassed at how to respond and all I could think of was to smile and wonder how they survived intact against the homophobic attitudes prevalent at that time.

That got me thinking about the prejudice about 'poofs' which most of us felt at the time but more so because they were so well mannered without being effeminate compared with the largely rough and ready mob which we had endured at the beginning of our tenure.

It was one of this pair of newcomers who explained to me that the word 'homo' had two meanings. From the Latin it means 'Man' and from the Greek, it means the 'same, similar or blending' as in homogeneous. Nonetheless, they were happy in their relationships and couldn't really understand why the majority of the population couldn't or wouldn't allow them to live their lives as they wished without harm to anybody else. But they were well aware that there was a very real hatred towards them from society at large.

Although I felt that I was reasonably balanced and fair minded towards this small group, I didn't want to have a reputation for the Dog and Partridge to be a pub catering especially for the underground homosexual community so I made some ground rules in quiet conversation with Gerald and Andrew (little did I know at the time of the extent of this sexual orientation in the area surrounding Mearsby!).

Speaking frankly to them at a private moment at the bar, I pleaded: 'You and your well behaved friends are very welcome and you can be sure that you will not be treated any differently from any other of our customers but please understand that the moment an overt, aggressive transvestite or straight dressing homosexual annoys one of my regulars, he will be banned instantly!'

'Oh Nick... How could you think such a thing of us or our friends. You've been so kind to us and we really do appreciate it because we love coming here for a drink and one of your lovely dinners but you really don't understand us do you? We'd never dream of doing anything like that. Do your straight friends start upsetting each other by "hitting" on the women in this place?' I had to do a rethink very quickly because I didn't want to lose them as friends or customers and suddenly realised that I was as prejudiced as everybody else.

It was an evening when Gerald and Andrew were

entertaining their friends when the boom dropped. Once again with my mastery of diplomacy I spotted the the most revolting transvestite. In my pub! And the house rules had been made quite clear.

She or He was dressed in a floral frock which certainly didn't match the masculine figure and the hair beneath the nose and the five o'clock shadow decorating the lantern jaw made me cringe. Lipstick had been strewn across the pair of large and heavy lips together with a pasting of rouge which had been rather crudely spread across the flabby cheeks. Any self respecting woman would never have gone out in public with such a foul hairdo. Her or his walking gait mimicked the style of a strong coal miner or farmer so I was convinced that we had an unashamed transvestite on our premises.

...This, I wouldn't put up with!

I was particularly put out as she/he was at the same table as Gerald and Andrew, and I had made it quite clear that they couldn't bring such people to our pub.

As I fulminated behind the bar, Enoch smirked and his grin grew wider as I told him that I was about to evict the loathsome creature. 'I would take yers time, m'boy,' he chortled.

'Things're not allus they seem, you mark me words.'

As he spoke, Gerald approached the bar to order another round and their meals. Before I could protest about his guest he gesticulated with a backward movement of his thumb towards the creature at his table and said: 'It's so nice to get my poor old mother out of the nursing home for a day or two. She's a bit batty these days, doesn't really know where she is but we thought she'd enjoy a little break and especially your kind and thoughtful hospitality.'

'We're going to give her a make-over tomorrow before we take her back.'

Enoch guffawed, Gerald looked mystified and I tried to hide my embarrassment whilst resolving to be more careful in future. Later, Enoch advised with a snigger. 'Yers 'ave two eyes, two ears, one brain 'n one mouth. Try usin' 'em in that order.' That was sound advice from an old campaigner!

A Funny Way to Run a Pub

The introduction of cask conditioned County Ale was an undoubted success. The only problem was that the beer was so strong that the majority of people couldn't drink more than a couple or so pints before being overwhelmed by the effects.

In fact, we had a standing (with apologies for the pun) challenge, that anybody who bought and drank six pints of County could have the seventh on the house. We rarely had to give away a pint on this basis although there were many who accepted the challenge and were generally helped home by their friends long before they were in striking distance of their prize. Many was the night when patrons' cars were locked up for the night in our car park for the safety of their owners, not to mention road users in general.

It became apparent that there was a great demand for 'ordinary' bitter to be available as Real Ale so we prevailed, once again, on Ruddles to supply us with another beer engine. In addition to the keg bitter we now had Ruddles 'sensible' cask conditioned beer which could be consumed in far greater quantities than the County Ale.

Clearly, this had to be marked by a celebration and our customers urged us to organise another silly event so a date was fixed for a fancy dress evening. All who arrived suitably attired would receive a free pint of bitter and a chance to win a hamper of country fare.

I dressed as a bishop complete with crook and mitre whilst my brother Charles undressed as Satan, a part to which he felt admirably suited. He wore black tights, painted his arms, chest and face blue and sported an enormous pair of papier mache horns.

Jane dressed as Long John Silver, but not having a parrot, she pinned a toy stuffed owl on her shoulder. Irene, who helped us with the catering, dressed as a Red Indian squaw whose head dress was made from genuine eagle feathers gathered from our chicken run.

Everything was set for a riotous evening when we opened and waited for the first merry makers.

Professor Sodd's law prevailed and the first customers to arrive were complete strangers. Needless to say, they knew nothing at all of the evening's arrangements and stared in blank amazement at the devil and bishop who grinned at them inanely from the other side of the bar.

It has never ceased to mystify me how the British seem to have the capability to ignore strange situations and people who do not immediately concern them and can remain unmoved in the most bizarre circumstances. So it was on this occasion.

Having recovered from his initial surprise, one of the group strode purposefully to the bar and ordered drinks from Charles as though nothing untoward was going on. Charles served him with a completely straight face. They then ordered a bar meal of scampi in the basket and were duly served by a feminine Long John Silver and an Indian squaw.

On finishing their food and drink, they thanked us for a pleasant meal and left. Not a word had been said about our clothes. No questions had been asked about the reasons for wearing them. Just blank acceptance.

That fancy dress evening was a tremendous success with people in the strangest costumes filling the bar, the car park and even overflowing into the lane that ran past the pub. Jane and I were presented with a 'Pub of the Year' award from a group of customers, Real Ale enthusiasts, who said that they had visited some 350 pubs in the previous year. Our little hostelry had been selected for no other reason than we were giving people what they wanted. It wasn't anything as grand as the 'Evening News' pub of the year award but nevertheless it was a very nice thought on the part of a group of dedicated barflies.

Well after closing time, two more customers arrived dressed very convincingly as policemen, much to the amusement of our hardcore drinkers. They fronted up to the bar, demanded that the music be turned down, people should be quiet and drink up and that the landlord was to be arrested for breach of the licensing laws. This was greeted by hoots of laughter and much abuse. A few seconds later it became obvious that these two were not in fancy dress. You could have cut the silence with a knife.

Ron and Cyril were at it again. Removing hats, radios and handcuffs, they sat at the bar and gazed around the room. 'Well don't just bloody stand there,' ordered Ron. 'Buy us a pint and hand me a guitar.'

He then proceeded to play and sing The St James Infirmary Blues.

He and Cyril were taking a tremendous risk with their careers but nobody ever said a word about the incident and I do believe that what they did that night achieved far more for police relations locally than could ever be imagined.

Business continued to grow steadily until we had one of the busiest pubs in the area. We were constantly visited by licensees of neighbouring pubs, most of whom were very friendly and somewhat taken aback by the speed with which we had managed to reverse the fortunes of our little hostelry.

I suppose we had proved a point. People, by and large, were always looking for an opportunity to let their hair down and didn't need much of an excuse to do so, especially in the relaxed atmosphere of a remote country pub. Our regular customers and especially the CAMRA groups that visited took a very real interest in how their beer was treated and kept. Provided we had the time to show them round, people had an open invitation to inspect the cellar and see for themselves how things were done. We couldn't see the point in keeping secret, the so called mystery of the landlord's art and it also ensured that there was no backsliding in the standards of cellar hygiene. No other landlord that we knew of was doing this and it was just another added attraction for Real Ale enthusiasts.

Such was the interest shown that we had no trouble in organising a party for an evening visit to the wonderful old Ruddles brewery just outside Oakham in Rutland. We were limited to a party of 25 and almost immediately after the announcement of the trip, it was over subscribed which led the disappointed to charge me, perhaps understandably, with being unable to organise a 'p... up in a brewery'. We hired a coach which was driven by none other than the Rev'd. Bob Vickers who was the aptly named rector of a neighbouring parish. He had become a regular customer over the previous months and was a devoted supporter of Real Ale. We secretly called him the 'Flashing Vicar'.

He would always visit us wearing a turtle necked pullover and whenever the jokes turned a little ripe, he would tug at the neck of his sweater to expose his dog collar in mock admonition. He had a part time job driving coaches to augment his slender stipend and a more down to earth, broad minded clergyman, you couldn't have wished to meet.

The enthusiastic brewery visitors met at the pub at 6.00pm and whetted their appetites with two pints each of County Ale. Everybody, that is except Bob Vickers whose driving responsibility prevented him from raising a glass until we were safely returned. In preparation for this, he had arranged for his wife, a very elegant lady, to come to the pub later in the evening in their camping van so that they could sleep over in the car park. We offered them a room for the night but they wouldn't hear of it.

On arrival at Ruddles, we were escorted to a huge cellar with a permanent bar built into it and presumably constructed for occasions such as this.

One of our number was co-opted as barman and for the following two hours, we were plied with the strongest ale that the brewery could offer. During that time, we were lectured on brewing methods old and new, the horrors of excise duty and the latest trends in the brewing industry. The free flow of ale ensured that our hosts had a captive, if somewhat glassy eyed audience after two hours of steady tippling.

When the first kilderkin had been exhausted, we were taken on a guided tour designed to illustrate the talk to which we should've been listening.

Words like mashtun, grist and wort took on a new meaning as our guide showed us the 'kettle'. This was a giant copper container in which the wort was boiled with the hops to extract the bitter flavour. We then staggered on to the 'Hop back' which was like a huge colander which strained most of the hop petals and other large solids from the wort after the boiling process.

Apparently the spent hop petals were used in the manufacture of cattle feed so there's a very obvious connection between milk and beer after all.

All of this was very interesting even through eyes dimmed by the earlier imbibing. Through yards, sheds, stores and bottling plants we trudged until we thought the tour was over, when, as if by magic, we were returned to the cellar bar where we were treated to another kilderkin of strong ale.

Poor old Bob. He had watched and listened his way through the entire visit without drinking more than a half pint of his favourite brew. What iron self control and Christian charity he showed to his fellow mankind that night.

George couldn't even remember the journey home and had to be escorted to his cottage where we left him propped up in the porch to await the ministrations of Mabel, his wife. We prudently retired from the scene before she opened the door to find George reeling incapably and singing merrily.

The good lady didn't speak to me for a week after that but I imagine that George had led her a merry dance that night. He always refused to talk about it, denying all knowledge of the event.

On our return to the pub, the survivors were all in party mood, none more so than Bob who was determined to try and catch up with the rest of us.

I had expected the pub to be rather quiet when we got back but the place was packed with a boisterous crowd, as drunk as we were and singing rugby songs at the top of their voices.

It was then that the awful truth struck!

I had agreed some weeks before that a local lad could hold his stag party on this particular night and had completely forgotten to tell Jane or Charles about it.

You can imagine that I wasn't Jane's favourite person at that time. She had spent the entire evening locked behind the bar refusing to come out into the main room as she was the only woman amongst the drunken crew. Fortunately, Charles was there to maintain some form of order but the pair of them were exhausted by the time we arrived.

Reinforcing the stag party with further hardened drinkers was a recipe for extreme high spirits and again, in breach of the law, continued until 4.00am.

There was a reversal of the normal turn of events at a stag party with Harry, the groom to be, having to look after Danny, his brother and best man who became totally and hopelessly drunk.

Apparently, Danny had tried to conspire with Jane so that every time Harry had a beer, she should put a vodka into it. She didn't want to do it but having been paid for the vodka, it would've been dishonest to withhold it. She doctored Danny's beer instead. Such was his condition that he fell out of the truck on the way home. He simply bounced on the road and suffered absolutely no ill effects whatever.

The following morning, with blazing hangovers, we invited Bob and his charming wife in from their camper for coffee.

The lady claimed to have slept soundly through the entire night but I know for a fact that at one stage there was a group of staggers drunkenly singing the ballad of Eskimo Nell in the middle of the car park, blissfully unaware of her presence.

It was Jane's birthday and we had gone out to celebrate, leaving Charles in charge of the bar with the usual instructions that if our regulars wanted to stay late, he should let them do so provided he felt like it.

We frequently had 'after hours' sessions which although they flew in the face of the licensing laws were harmless and those who were welcome to stay were people whose company we enjoyed and in other circumstances would've been invited to our home. The main difference was that they paid for their drinks. Good company or not we couldn't afford to be philanthropists.

There was never any trouble at or around the pub as a result of these sessions and we felt quite comfortable in the knowledge that our local bobby and his partner were largely turning a blind eye to our activities. From time to time, we'd receive an 'anonymous' telephone call from a guardian angel simply saying: 'Keep a good house tonight.'

We always respected this advice and took it to mean that

the local sergeant or the County police would be on the prowl after 10.30pm. On these occasions, we always closed on time with the full co-operation of our locals.

When Jane and I returned from her birthday dinner at about midnight in excellent spirits, we found about a dozen people who with Charles, were obviously enjoying themselves.

John who was six feet seven inches tall and built like an all in wrestler called to me in a slurring voice: 'Wanna drink Nick?'

'Thanks John,' I replied. 'I've had enough beer though. A scotch and soda would be good.'

John handed me the whisky. 'Here's your scotch and here's your soda.'

WH00000SH!

All I saw was a stream of froth curling towards me and John's lower jaw dropping in a drunken laugh. I was soaked from head to foot as he emptied the entire siphon at me. The place was in uproar. Raucous laughter filled the room as bodies banged into each other and hands slapped backs as they fought to control themselves. I made a lunge at the other soda siphon on the bar but John beat me to it yelling: 'Have at thee Sir!' as he fired again but this time the spray hit the bar door as I leapt through and slammed it behind me. In the room behind the bar was a crate of six soda siphons and as far as I was concerned, every one had John's name on it.

I re-entered the bar with a bottle in each hand, spraying as I went. Amid the shouts of laughter, things suddenly went wrong. John threw his 16 stone bulk behind Bernard's father for cover but in the excitement, I kept spraying. Poor old Mr Jenkins. He caught one jet full in the face and the other in his left ear.

His laughter suppressed, he stood up, shook himself like a wet dog and declared: 'Tha's the last bloody toim I use this pub. Yers all bloody ravin' mad, yer stupid buggers. Buggers tha's what yers are. Mad stupid buggers.'

He did come back though and I apologised to him for his soaking. We became the best of friends again but whenever the late night sessions became lively, he and his wife were the first to leave and I suppose I couldn't blame him for that.

Music plays an important part wherever you have a group of people intent on enjoying themselves. Our stereo system provided background music but was never a real feature of the place except when it went haywire, playing LPs at 50rpm making Louis Armstrong sound like he had overdosed on helium.

It did come in handy on one occasion when we had a surprise visit by about 30 bikers, many of whom were under age.

Rather than risk a confrontation, I simply played The Planets by Holst at high volume. The effect was instantaneous. Not a word had been said, but they either finished or left their drinks and swiftly departed.

Our musician friend, Conor, was keen to play the piano occasionally and although we liked the idea, we didn't have space in the bar to put one because of the number of people who would crowd into the place.

Eventually a great British compromise was worked out.

We had a honky-tonk piano in one of the out buildings and agreed that on sunny Sunday lunchtimes we'd haul it out into the garden where Conor could play to his heart's content.

This obviously appealed to a lot of people because once the word had gone round, they beat a path to our door to enjoy Conor's music and their drinks out in the warm sunshine.

What had started as a joke became a Sunday lunch spectacular when Conor's seven year old son Sean accompanied his father with a precocious and very competent performance on drums. The idea started to snowball and before we knew it, people were bringing their own musical instruments and at one time we had an impromptu 10 piece band playing on the lawn.

Oiled with County ale, many would be singers lent their own particular talents. Surprisingly, the overall quality of the music was very good indeed, witnessed by the fact that not one villager complained.

From one end of the village to the other, throughout that long hot summer of 1976, music could be heard nearly every Sunday between 12.00 and 2.00pm and very often much later than that.

During the week, Conor would occasionally sit in the bar, playing a mandolin, guitar or clarinet. One evening three of his friends turned up unexpectedly, complete with tin whistle, guitar and fiddle and provided a superb performance of Irish folk music to the delight of our customers. Within half an hour of their starting to play, the lounge was packed with appreciative listeners who had presumably heard the news on the bush telegraph.

Conor and his friends performed several times but always unexpectedly and on each occasion, the pub would fill, but then Conor and friends were very good musicians who were as happy playing at the Dog and Partridge simply for the sheer enjoyment as they were when playing at packed theatres in the cities.

I never ceased to be amazed at the cross section of our society who attended these evenings and mixed so freely that you'd have thought that they were lifelong friends.

There were all ages from 18 to 80 comprised of farm workers, doctors, vets, land owners, lawyers, builders, shopkeepers, dustmen and often the odd titled gentleman of whom there were many in this part of the country.

Sociologists may tell you about the different socio-economic strata whose social lives are firmly anchored within their own group. Had they attended the only public room at our pub, especially when the musicians were there, then I suspect they'd have been tempted to re-think their theories, such was the diversity of trades, professions and intellects on most evenings.

Having put the Dog and Partridge on the map, we were by now enjoying a huge increase in trade and turned our thoughts to what else we could do to keep the momentum going.

It seemed to me that every time Jane and I did something different or at least, against the trend of 'modernisation', we attracted more and more customers and although this created a tremendous workload for Jane, Charles and I, it was of course our very reason for being there.

We had a very scruffy lean-to at the back of the pub whose timber walls were reasonably solid but whose roof was constructed of light weight corrugated plastic. Barney had demonstrated how weak it was by leaping right through it in pursuit of a bird. It was a draughty, damp and rather unpleasant room which had previously been used as a village shop of sorts but had long since fallen into disrepair.

We didn't see ourselves as village shopkeepers but nonetheless decided to re-build the room. We were sure that with the ever increasing number of customers, we could find a use for it.

By scrounging most of the materials such as corrugated panels for the roof and insulated lining for the walls, we were able to restore the lean-to as a comfortable and warm ante-room.

Throughout the county, the traditional game of skittles was dying out as more country pubs succumbed to modernisation through provision of 'restaurants', discos and the like.

As our pub was being run on traditional lines, we decided to install an old skittles table in the lean-to with a view to reviving interest in the game.

Northamptonshire Skittles is a very noisy and exciting game but because of the location of the lean-to, we were confident that there wouldn't be too much disturbance in the lounge. We were also lucky that there was a hatchway from the bar to the new room which would allow us to serve drinks to the players.

We acquired an old table from a pub in Rushford and had it renovated by a local upholsterer and before long we were in the Skittles business. We had a feeling that it would prove to be popular and would add more character to our little hostelry but little did we know what we were letting ourselves in for.

The traditional skittles table or board is mounted on a sturdy framework supported by four very heavy turned wooden legs. The playing surface stands about two feet nine inches above the floor. The board itself is made from solid timber covered with cow hide which is kept highly polished. On each side of the board are two timber walls which are heavily padded with horsehair and also covered with cow hide. Rising from the back to form a protective 'roof' is a rope mesh hood which also wraps around the sides above the 'walls' to a certain extent. Many a broken head has been avoided by the protection against flying pins and cheeses provided by this hood. It's this piece of equipment which lends its name to the alternative title of the game — Hood skittles.

On the board itself, in a diamond formation, are placed nine skittles or 'pins'. These were traditionally made from extremely hard wood but were gradually being replaced with a hard plastic compound. Made from the same material as the pins, were three 'cheeses' measuring about three and a half inches in diameter and one and a half inches thick. These 'cheeses', known as balls were thrown by the players from a distance of about nine feet, at the pins with a view to knocking down as many as possible.

If all nine pins were knocked down with one ball, this was known locally as a 'floorer'.

There was a tradition that if the maximum score of 27 was made, then the landlord gave a cigar to the player concerned. Where this tradition came from, I have no idea but not once did I have to give away a cigar, such was the difficulty of this particular achievement.

When nine pins were bowled over by two balls, this was known as a 'stack up' simply because the pins had to be stacked up again for the player to make his third and final throw.

Scoring, according to the rules of the league in which we eventually competed, was easy, once you had seen it in action.

Two teams of seven people each compete in a match. A player's picked from each side by lot to play his opposite number which results in seven games involving two players taking place. Each game was known as a 'horse'. Each match consisted of seven 'horses' contested by 14 players.

Each 'horse' was contested as follows:

One player threw his three balls and his score was noted whilst his opponent attempted to beat the score he had been set by one point. In the event of a draw, the second player in the drawn 'horse' simply threw one ball at nine pins to reach a score which his opponent then attempted to beat with one ball by one point.

In the event that the 'one ball' was drawn, the players continued alternately with one ball until the point was decided. The first player to win seven 'horses' won the game.

When the seven games had been played out, the winning team was the one to have won most horses.

It was as simple as that but trying to explain the rules to visitors perhaps 10 times in an evening became very wearing but, fortunately there was usually a regular player on hand to show them the basics.

In no time at all, there was a hardcore of people playing skittles every night. Their skills at the game varied enormously but all were extremely enthusiastic including Danny of Stag party fame.

Danny's brother, Tom was the secretary of a nearby sports and social club and at Danny's behest, suggested a Grand Challenge night.

In addition to the skittle table, we had a creaky old bar-billiards table and an equally ancient shove ha' penny board so we decided to include these games for the night. The idea of the Pub Games Tournament was born and the word went round. The response was staggering and we mustered 32 players plus a healthy number of cheer leaders whilst the challengers from the sports and social club raised a similar number.

This meant over 60 people who wanted to play three separate games making a total of over 90 games if they played in pairs. We decided that each game should be played by two pairs but even then we realised that the law would be broken again that night as the games would take at least four hours to complete and that we couldn't reasonably start until 8.00pm. Such were and still are the restrictions imposed by our antiquated licensing laws.

We got underway at 8.30 with the teams most undemocratically selected by simply taking their names in the order that they arrived at the bar. The same teams battled with each other on all three pieces of equipment and were scored by John, the giant of soda siphon fame.

Such was his size that nobody argued about his decisions and his scoring method was simple enough. Two points for a win, one point each for a draw.

The heat generated by the crowd's exertion together with the cheering and shouting was unbelievable, as was their capacity for beer. Charles and I changed five 18 gallon kilderkins that night to keep the ale flowing.

At 11.00pm, half an hour after official closing time, the games were only halfway through and the excitement and tempo, if anything, was still rising.

'Might as well get hung for a sheep as a lamb.' I thought as I turned off the outside lights and drew the curtains in a vain attempt to conceal what was going on inside.

The tournament continued until 1.00am when I rang the bell for the announcement of the result. John's bull voice rang out: 'The two sides were so evenly matched that the result's a draw.'

Amid the shouting and cheering, I examined his score sheet and noticed two names with scores next to them that were obviously fictitious. 'What are you up to John?' I asked. 'These two weren't even here tonight.'

'I know,' he replied. 'The scores were pretty close but in the social club's favour. I thought if we had a draw, then Tom would challenge you to a return match.'

No sooner had he said it than Tom appeared at the bar. 'A great night Nick. If it's alright by you, we'll be back in two weeks time for the return and then two weeks after that for the decider.'

'You're on!' I said rather quickly, thinking more about the beer and catering sales which the evening had produced.

Perhaps John's action, if a little villainous, was a good idea after all.

The evening was repeated twice and the social club deservedly won the series but that didn't matter to our players. It was the opportunity to let their hair down that counted and they certainly knew how to do that.

The idea of the tournament caught on and not a week went by without at least one skittling event where we either participated or simply played host to different groups but I always tried to keep the numbers down to a maximum of 40 players. We may have been accustomed to late nights but we couldn't keep up the pace indefinitely.

'Can't we get into a league?' asked Big Danny — so named by the locals because of his girth rather than his height. He had a voice and a laugh as big as his waistline and although he was in his early 20s had emerged as the skittler's leader not so much because of any real skill at the game but more because of his hearty approach to it and his seemingly boundless enthusiasm.

Unknown to Danny and the others I had already found a

suitable league where the playing standard wasn't too high and the sociability of the majority of its members was excellent. The last thing we wanted was people taking the game too seriously and thereby losing sight of the real reason for playing; an entertaining and noisy night out.

Danny called a meeting where he was unanimously voted as Team Captain and the decision was taken to join a league.

One month later at the league's Annual General Meeting, the Dog and Partridge was welcomed as the newest member and placed in the second division where, to the best of my knowledge, it has always remained.

Our first away game was played at the 'Cow and Calf', a small pub on the other side of the river. Our team set out in high spirits determined to make an impression. Unfortunately, Jane and I couldn't accompany them that night as we had a party organised at the pub so Charles went along as a player.

They returned at about 10.00pm in a high state of excitement.

'We won, We won,' they cried. 'It was easy,' yelled Big Danny. 'I reckon we'll do quite well in this league.'

Buying drinks all round, Jane and I congratulated them on their performance. We were genuinely pleased.

Their winning streak didn't last however. The 'Cow and Calf' was the only team they beat in the entire season.

Were they downhearted? Not a bit of it. There was always the following season to notch up a victory.

The vast majority of the teams in the league, played for the same reason as us; to have a good night out, but there were exceptions amongst the individuals involved.

On one occasion, amongst the visitors was a crab-faced woman in her 50s whose attitude matched her looks. Her first comment on entering the pub was: 'Skittle room's too bloody small. Shouldn't be allowed in the league.' She didn't so much ask for her drinks but demand them but I had become a lot more tolerant of ill mannered people by this time as we saw so little of them.

One of our younger players, Bert by name, really let this woman get under his skin. She was drawn to play against him and her constant barrage of complaints and moaning, finally became too much for him. Turning to the visiting team captain, he burst out: 'Why the hell d'you put up with her? The bloody woman should be shot to put her out of her misery!'

'I couldn't agree with you more my boy,' he replied. 'And I should know. I've been married to her for the past 30 years.' Bert, crimson with embarrassment fled from the skittle room and sought refuge amongst the crowd in the lounge.

We had lost the last league game of the season and been knocked out of all the competitions but for all that had enjoyed a thoroughly entertaining winter. There was one thing left to play for. The wooden spoon which was contested between us and the lowest scoring side in the first division. We ended up empty handed, having been beaten by a far superior team. At the end of season dinner and celebration, Big Danny stood up to make his speech which included the stirring words: 'Never fear, lads and lassies. We may not be the most successful team in the league but we're certainly the strongest. Have a look at the team placings. We're holding up all the others.' Danny was re-elected again unanimously, as captain for the following season.

It was Danny, with his usual exuberance who suggested that we should enter a team for the annual Stilton Cheese Rolling competition sponsored by the 'Stilton Cheese' pub in the village of the same name not far from Peterborough.

'Good idea,' said the giant John. 'Put me down and I'll get my little brother to join in.'

I thought about his little brother who was in fact a good four inches taller than John and probably about two stones heavier.

A plan began to form in my mind. 'Right we'll do it. You three, Bernard and myself. There's not one of us under six feet tall and we'll call ourselves the "Mearsby Midgets".'

Over several pints of beer, we discussed our plan of action to win the competition. There had to be something that we could win!

The Stilton Cheese Rolling competition has its origins shrouded in mystery. Some say it dates back to the time when the Melton Mowbray to London stagecoach used to stop in the village for overnight accommodation for its passengers and no doubt the famous cheeses were rolled off the coach for local consumption. It's said that when the cheeses were loaded at Melton for London that the dairymen's' cry was: 'Here's the Stilton Cheese', in recognition of the coach's first overnight stop.

One thing I know for certain is that Stilton cheese has never been made in Stilton but I suppose that every village needs some claim to fame.

Local cynics will tell you that the competition isn't at all ancient but has only recently been invented.

Whatever its origins, it was held at 11.00am on Easter Sunday every year and raised substantial funds for charity.

It was a colourful, totally insane spectacle guaranteed to make you laugh but nonetheless was contended very seriously by the many pub teams and others who entered for the chance of winning a whole Stilton cheese and two crates of beer.

If you have the opportunity, it's well worth a visit and costs you nothing to watch. The organisers depend entirely on the audience's generosity when the collecting tins come round.

Each team consists of a minimum of three and a maximum of six people, all in fancy dress whose task is to roll a 'cheese' over a prepared route of about 100 yards of Stilton High Street and to cross the finishing line ahead of their competitors.

It sounds simple enough.

The 'cheese' is a section of tree trunk about the same size as a true Stilton cheese and is never perfectly round. It never rolls in a straight line. The rules stipulated that the cheese should never leave the ground and any team who threw it would be disqualified.

It was a knockout competition and the teams competed three at a time with the winners going through to the next round until there were only two teams left to compete in the final. The 'Mearsby Midgets' arrived on the scene variously clad in pink candy striped boiler suits and hard hats, as a pirate, Santa Claus and a clown. We hadn't had time to coordinate the outfits.

Looks of fear appeared on the faces of some of our competitors as they gazed with disbelief at our size and combined weight of over 75 stones.

In the event, they needn't have been concerned.

We may have done justice in the front row of a Rugby 15 but as we were to find out, our height was a considerable hindrance in a cheese rolling competition. Quite simply, we couldn't reach the ground as quickly as our smaller competitors.

John had trouble keeping a low profile but his brother, Tim was downright comical as he tried to run doubled over, looking very much like an elephant with a hernia.

By some stroke of good fortune, we managed to reach the semi finals where we were drawn against a bunch of fairies.

A short bearded man in Wellington boots, tights and a sequined shirt with gossamer wings sprouting from his back was teamed up with two very slight 10 year old girls. It must've been hilarious to watch five hulking great men clumsily tripping over each other and ending up in a mass of tangled limbs in their forlorn attempt to stave off defeat by the two dainty little girls and their bearded fairy godmother.

We left Stilton empty handed after the prize giving ceremony and headed for the Dog and Partridge.

Having washed away the bitter taste of ignominious defeat with a few pints of County ale, I ventured: 'What about next year?'

'Not on yer bloody life,' replied Tim. 'Oi've decided oim a watcher, not a doer.'

'We could always form a tug of war team,' I suggested. Under the threat of being thrown into the nearby brook by these brooding giants, I withdrew the idea.

Feather, Fur and Folklore

The furthest we ever ventured into the field of stock keeping was with our hens and rabbits.

Needless to say, both George and Enoch were very forthcoming with advice on how to get the best from them. I tried to explain that the rabbits were pets, for the entertainment of our customers and definitely not for the table.

How on earth could you make a meal out of animals called Flopsy, Big Ears and their offspring Castor and Pollux, the identical twins.

The two old countrymen couldn't see the point in having rabbits simply for the pleasure of keeping them and never missed a chance to tell us how delicious was roast tame rabbit. We suspected however, that these comments were made purely for devilment. The rabbits, in their large enclosure, provided hours of entertainment for our customers' children who were happy to spend time in the gardens whilst their parents enjoyed the traditional pleasures of a country pub.

The chickens of which we had 20 were kept for another purpose; egg production.

George and Enoch's advice here was invaluable and I am sure that without it, our egg supply and continued survival of the birds would've been severely limited.

The expression 'killing with kindness' was never more true than with our treatment of the hens shortly after they had arrived. Two of them died, for no apparent reason, one after the other and we simply couldn't understand it.

They had a large wired enclosure and their roosts were under cover in a draught proofed area. We provided a plentiful fresh water supply and significantly, as it turned out, plenty of food and grit.

I told Enoch about the problem and he agreed to come along and see the birds at feeding time.

'Morning or Afternoon?' I asked. 'By the left! You don't feed 'em twice a day do yers? That's it m'boy. Tha' would be yer answer. Oi'll come this afternoon 'n see 'em.'

Twice a day, in my supreme ignorance, I had been mixing up a large quantity of layers mash plus a tin full of mixed corn and any grass or weeds to feed our domesticated vultures as we liked to call them, and not without reason. They, like all hens were incredibly greedy and amidst a great squawking and swearing they'd demolish all the available food within minutes.

'M'boy,' said Enoch on arrival at the chicken run. 'Them birds is overfed. Them's getting crop bound. Tha's the problem wi' the dead uns. if yers want eggs, yers gotta make 'em work fer their grub. Four ounces a bird a day. Tha's all they need an' scatter it around. Make 'em scratch fer it an' I'll tell yers summat else. Don't waste yers money on special grit. Coal ash. Tha's the stuff fer 'em. Chuck it in every day 'n they'll peck what they need and bath in the rest. Tha's guaranteed ter keep off the mites.'

'By the left! you townies know 'ow ter waste yers money!'

As usual, he was right on all counts. We followed his advice to the letter and within a few weeks, the birds had settled down and were producing large tasty eggs as regular as clockwork.

George solved the next problem.

The birds had been pecking at each other and pulling out their own feathers to such an extent that I thought it was some sort of avian death wish. Some of them looked oven-ready.

Having asked for George's opinion, he had a good look around the chicken run and house.

'Soon fix that,' he said and went back to his cottage. He returned with some very old, large and rusty metal cans.

'Throw out them galvanised trows. They'm no good. Yers need a good bit o' iron. That's their trouble boy. Need more iron. Allus use old cans fer their water; the rustier the better. It'll be orlright now. Jes wait 'n see. It'll be orlright.'

We swapped the water containers and he said: 'It's jes' knowing what t'do, a vet would've charged yers good money fer tha' bit o' advice.'

'Point taken George,' I replied. 'You'd better come into the bar and I'll settle your account right now.'

He needed no urging and over his second pint, I told him my other worry about the birds.

'For the last two nights, we've had a fox around the run. I've heard him coughing and scratching outside. Is there anything I can do about it?'

'Yers could allus shoot the bugger if yers saw 'im,' mused George with a twinkle in his eye.

He knew how I felt about killing foxes even if they didn't extend the same sentiment towards my chickens.

'No. George,' I replied. 'There's few enough of them in their natural habitat as it is. I just want to keep him away from the chickens because if he did succeed in getting in, he'd probably go berserk and kill the lot.'

'Mmm,' mumbled George handing me his empty glass for a refill. 'Yers could allus loose a button there.'

'Loose a button George? What on earth d'you mean?' I replied in all innocence and still unaware of all the local expressions. He guffawed as only he knew how.

'Y'silly bugger. Pee! Loose a button an' pee roun' the run. Dogs do it t'mark their own territories. Why shouldn' yers? It'd work oi should think.'

Without admitting it to anybody, that night, full of beer, I followed George's advice and later still when all was quiet in the village, I heard the fox close by again.

That however, was the last time that I heard him near the run and although it could be that he had simply given up with the hens, I like to think that it was George's country remedy that had done the trick.

If the fox had given up, our daft dog Houdini most certainly hadn't. Not that there was anything malicious in his never ending attempts to get in amongst the hens. It was straightforward mischief and a single minded desire to be somewhere forbidden to him.

Anyone who owns an English Setter will know exactly what I mean.

His first assault on the run was straightforward enough. A tunnel under the wire. The first inkling we had that something was wrong was when one of the villagers' children knocked on the door to tell us that one of our hens was trapped in a holly bush just outside the pub. I looked, and sure enough, the poor creature had flown into the bush and was trapped by the prickly leaves and branches as securely as if she were in a cage. I rescued her at the personal cost of lacerated hands and forearms, revived her with a drop of brandy and returned her to the run.

The sight that met my eyes there made me angry at the time although it's funny to think back on.

Houdini was fast asleep on the straw in the roosting house with not a chicken to be seen anywhere. Their escape was made through the tunnel which he had dug under the wire.

With the dog severely told off and skulking in the far corner of the garden, we repaired the wire and filled in the tunnel. We then set about rounding up the hens and within about half an hour, they were safely returned to their run.

One hour later, a frantic squawking alerted us to further trouble. Houdini was at it again. His method was the same but the site was different. We caught him wriggling under the wire just as his rear end was disappearing into the tunnel. It was a perfect irresistible target which I struck with the flat of my hand as sharply and quickly as I could.

He yelped, more from surprise than anything else. The only pain inflicted was on my hand.

Naturally, he was very sorry about his crime, grovelling and fawning at my feet, his huge floppy ears drawn back and his eyes full of anguish as he raised first one paw then another in what can only be described as abject apology. I wasn't going to be taken in by this performance.

'Right dog,' I said. 'If you like being in a cage so much we'll put you in one.' With that we marched him off to the old outside ladies toilets and shut him in solitary confinement just for a few minutes. It was there that he made a discovery which was to plague us for months afterwards but we'll come to that later.

We decided to reinforce the chicken run by means of paving slabs and heavy stones around the perimeter to stop the hound from digging his way in. After his punishment, he was well aware that the hens were out of bounds to him and whenever Jane or I went into the garden, Houdini would make sure that he was well away from their run. Unknown to us, of course, he was planning another way to break in.

If you feel that the word 'planning' suggests that Houdini was able to consider and solve problems you would be absolutely right. Believe me, in spite of their lunatic appearance and behaviour, English Setters are extremely intelligent. Too intelligent for their own and their owners well being.

I had just fed the birds and was on my way back to the house when that, by now, familiar hysterical squawking alerted me to further trouble.

I got to the run in time to see Houdini racing around inside the wire and the poor old hens, who were by now well off the lay, jumping and flying out of the hole in the wire. This time he had made a really good job of it. Undeterred by the slabs and the stones, he had simply bitten through the wire and enlarged the hole with his paws. My patience was running out with the dog.

Another clip across the rump, another bawling out, the inevitable canine apology followed by another short spell in solitary confinement seemed to me to be a reasonable way to get through to Houdini. Subsequent events proved me wrong.

Discussing the problem in the bar one night with George,

who knew a thing or two about dogs, I was advised to bite Houdini's ear next time he committed a crime. 'Tha's what a dog pack leader does in the wild if any of the young uns gerrout o' hand. Doan yers bite 'im too 'ard though, jes a nip on t'end o' 'is ear t'let 'im know who's boss.'

I decided to try at the very next opportunity which naturally enough wasn't too long in presenting itself.

We had reinforced the wire of the run with some 'bite proof' steel mesh scrounged from Enoch and were convinced that the hens were now secure against invasion. How wrong we were.

We hadn't padlocked the door into the run and Houdini, no doubt after careful observation, had simply lifted the latch and let the chickens out that way.

This had to be the final straw. I bellowed at him. He grovelled. I bit his ear. He yelped and off we went to the ladies toilet.

There was one further attack on the chicken run after that but on this occasion, Houdini had managed to move one of the stones at the base of the wire and reverted to his old trick of tunnelling. Obviously the nip on the ear had been no more effective than a clout on the rump. Or had it? This time the dog had learnt something. Instead of his apologetic grovelling, he bounded up to me, offered his ear to be bitten and without a sound rushed off to the ladies loo and shut himself in solitary confinement.

I never nipped his ear after that but if we ever found him in the ladies, we knew that he was punishing himself and that somewhere we'd find evidence of yet another crime.

He never failed to disappoint us in this respect.

It was shortly after this episode that Houdini decided that breaking out of the pub gardens to the great world beyond, was much more fun than breaking into the chicken run. Previously it hadn't seemed to worry him that he was enclosed by walls and fences and had made no attempt to jump them until some sheep took up residence in the adjacent field. The sight and smell of them must have been too much for him as he cleared the fence at a single bound and was in amongst what I am sure he took to be woolly playmates. Unfortunately the sheep didn't view him with the same outlook and immediately panicked, tearing every which way in their attempts to avoid him.

We managed to get him back before the sheep were entirely exhausted by his efforts to play with them and I was extremely relieved to find that none of them was in lamb at the time. Following a scolding, he put himself in solitary confinement having again offered me his ear which, with some misgiving, I refused to bite.

It was the incident with the sheep that prompted us to turn the pub gardens into a mini Colditz and raise the height of the walls and fences with heavy duty steel netting which had been kindly donated by Mr Ford who owned the sheep.

Our other problem was the gateway which was blocked when the pub was closed by a rather flimsy wooden gate which Houdini had demolished in a headlong charge which had taken him straight through it in his quest for freedom.

Clearly the gate had to be replaced. Charles and I were to find out that gate building was the prerogative of the true countryman and although no offers of actual help were given during its construction, Enoch, George and Wilf did try to persuade us that as it wasn't built by them, it would never survive the first winter gale.

The timber which we used had been found in an outhouse where it had lain for many years. Huge baulks of old oak of varying lengths and thicknesses were eventually sorted out and cut to the required size for assembly. Crude joints were made and the whole thing was hammered together using six inch nails. Hinges and hangers were scrounged from Mr Brent and at last we were able to hang the new gate. Amidst good natured jeers and abuse from the villagers and Wilf in particular, our massive, five barred, diagonally supported gate was heaved onto its supports and much to our surprise, after the barracking we had received, swung to and fro perfectly with no sign of sagging along its nine foot length. Admittedly, it did look strange in Northamptonshire with its hinge post being two feet six inches higher than the top rail and with a huge metal strap joining the top of that post to the shorter post at the latch end but it was, dare I say it, designed to be functional and Houdini proof rather than traditional.

As we stood back amongst the somewhat quieter villagers to admire our handiwork, the retired army colonel who lived on the edge of the village appeared on horseback. 'That's an improvement on the old one,' he declared. 'Fine strong looking gate that. What! What! Know a thing or two about gates myself. That's a Scottish design. What! Should last for donkeys years.'

With that, he rode off leaving Charles and I grinning with self-satisfaction at Wilf and company who were now examining the gate from a more approving and somewhat less jaundiced viewpoint. The Colonel never knew how his timely comments raised Charles and I as gate builders, in the esteem of the locals.

'If you spent a bit more time with him, he probably wouldn't be so naughty,' said Jane. 'He's only asking for your attention. You know he thinks the world of you though God only knows why. You really ought to let him follow you around the place to let him know that you're really interested in him.'

I only half heard what she was saying as I was fulminating over Houdini's latest campaign of terror. Ever since his first period of solitary confinement when he discovered the pleasures of chewing up toilet rolls he had, every day taken to stealing the rolls and decorating the gardens and car park with giant streamers and occasionally bringing me the cardboard tube from the centre as if to claim responsibility for the havoc he was causing. There seemed to be no way that I could teach the dog the error of his ways.

I agreed to Jane's suggestion but with a feeling of foreboding which as things turned out was fully justified.

That day, I proposed to visit Ruddles wine and spirit depot to replenish our stocks and, deciding to take Houdini with me, made an uneventful journey.

On arrival, the dog, apparently asleep, ignored me when I lifted the tailgate of the estate car and I took out some empty crates in which to carry out the stock which I intended to buy. Shutting the back of the car, I left him snoozing and went down into Ruddles cellars.

'Hey you!' a voice shouted. 'You can't bring your dog in here.'

Turning round, I saw to my horror, Houdini silently padding along behind me then suddenly turning into a streak of orange and white lightning as he raced towards the spirits department where something had caught his attention. Cursing my negligence for not checking that the tailgate was securely fastened, I dropped the crates and went after him. 'Whatever you do, don't chase him.' I yelled; but it was too late. The blood chilled in my veins as I saw two white coated attendants giving chase as the dog leapt with excitement over displays of expensive malt whisky. 'For God's sake stop chasing him,' I bellowed. 'He'll tear the place apart.'

The two men stopped as Houdini skidded around a stack of brandy bottles and came to a halt with his front legs flat on the floor and his rear end up, his tail wagging furiously and dangerously close to half a dozen bottles of Cointreau.

'Sit and stay.' I roared at him and to my surprise, his front end came up as his hind quarters touched the ground. As I walked quickly towards him, one of the attendants crept up behind him.

'Gotcha,' he said as his hand grabbed the empty space in front of him, Houdini having leapt away at the sound of the man's approach.

'You bloody fool. Now look what you've done.' I cried, almost shedding tears of rage and frustration as the dog raced off towards the wine department. My only consolation was that the destruction of a few crates of wine would cost me a lot less than shattered bottles of spirits and liqueurs.

His escape to the wine department was also his undoing as that area was a honeycomb of nooks and crannies which led from a central corridor and he was finally cornered, barking furiously, in a small vault sporting the sign.' Vintage ports Please do not disturb.'

Grabbing him by the collar, I led him back to the car and imprisonment, making sure that the doors were firmly locked and Houdini proof. Miraculously, not a bottle had been broken during his escapade and I heaved a sigh of relief at my escape from potential bankruptcy. 'Give him another chance,' said Jane. 'It wasn't really his fault. Why don't you take him into the cellar with you when you clean the beer lines. He can't do much harm there can he?'

All went smoothly as I performed the task with Houdini padding along behind me whenever I moved and sitting quietly next to me, showing a great interest in what I was doing as I stripped and cleaned the beer engines. For a moment I thought that he was a reformed character but experience tempered my charitable outlook.

'This just has to be the calm before the storm,' I mused. 'This hound is planning his next assault.' I could almost see it in his eyes but foolishly ignored the warning signs.

We descended to the cellar.

When a fresh barrel has been tapped, you have to draw off a pint or so of beer direct from the cask to ensure that the tap itself is clear of any sediment and the beer is ready for serving before you connect the tap to the beer line. I was in the process of doing just that when the tap became jammed in the 'on' position. Undeterred, I stuck my thumb up the spout to stop the flow and reached for the wrench to turn it off.

Houdini, that spotty horror, was sitting in the far corner of the cellar with the wrench gripped firmly between his jaws. I could have sworn that he was laughing at me. 'Here Boy. Fetch it.' I called but got no response. I tried cajoling, coaxing and wheedling to no effect. I then tried cursing and shouting but he just sat there enjoying the spectacle of his 'master' unable to leave the barrel, rather like the little Dutch boy Henrik with his finger in the dyke. Eventually, tiring of the game, he dropped the wrench and ran up the cellar steps and away.

There was nothing for it but to leave the barrel and make a dash for the wrench.

With the tap turned off, I counted the cost. Nervous exhaustion, high blood pressure and at least one gallon of beer down the drain. The dog was becoming a threat to my sanity.

Stubbornly, I persevered and wherever I went or whatever I did, Houdini could be seen in attendance. When he was behaving himself he was the most charming, appealing and amusing companion I could have wished to have but his crimes over the next few days nearly broke my will to live.

He stole the wallet from my back pocket and chewed it to shreds but by some fortunate chance, the bank notes had dropped out and escaped his attention.

He chewed and ate the fresh plaster with which I had just repaired a large area of wall in the cellar. This was a habit which he repeated whenever Walter, the builder came to perform repair work except that he had also developed a taste for wet mortar. Walter felt that a liberal coating of Colmans fresh mustard on top of the plaster would deter the dog. He was wrong. Houdini simply ate it with relish before attacking the soft plaster beneath.

He stole and destroyed a paperback from the bookshelf. I knew he was intelligent but was surprised to see that the book he had chosen was Gerald Durrell's: My Family and Other Animals. I couldn't turn my back on him for five minutes without some minor disaster occurring. Eventually I had to admit defeat and end the experiment of close attention.

'Let him loose in the yard and garden again,' I said to Jane. 'I just can't take any more.'

Things got back to normal after that with Houdini going his way and me going mine. He was too expensive in terms of material damage and wear and tear on my nervous system to be with me all day. Security and peace of mind were bought at the cost of about 10 toilet rolls a week. A small price to pay for sanity.

'We're going away for a short while, maybe for three weeks to record some music and to give Conor and the kids a break,' said Anne,. 'And we wondered if you would mind keeping an eye on the animals for us.'

'No problem at all,' I replied thinking of her two beautiful Samoyed dogs and her rather nondescript cat. 'I'll pop in and feed them once a day and take them for a walk with Houdini.'

She looked at me with a rather puzzled expression on her face. 'There's no need for that, just make sure that their chains are secure and move them from time to time.'

'Chains?' I said. 'You can't keep those lovely dogs chained up for three weeks.' 'Not the dogs. They're coming with us. I mean the goats!'

'Oh no, not another trip into the unknown.' I thought.

I knew nothing about goats but was assured that there was nothing to it. All I had to do was check their chains and move them around so that they could crop fresh grass.

'Sounds simple enough. Yes of course Anne... we'll see to them. You enjoy your holiday and don't worry about the goats. They'll be looked after.' I said with more conviction than I felt.

There were three things that she hadn't told me. Felicity, the nanny goat was pregnant.

Desmond, the billy goat, was an evil smelling, rheumy eyed monster whose sole purpose in life seemed to be the wholesale destruction of the human race.

The holiday would last for six weeks not three.

The day after Conor and Anne had left, I visited their cottage and everything seemed to be in order. Both the goats were securely tethered and had plenty of grass left in their respective circles so I merely topped up their water troughs and left although I fancied that I had seen a rather malevolent look in Desmond's eyes. Putting it down to inexperience and imagination, I thought no more about it.

A couple of days later, they were ready for their first move and, pulling out Felicity's anchor pin, I led her to pastures new. That was when I made my first mistake. Walking slowly across Desmond's area, I turned my back on him. All I felt was a sharp thump in the back and I lay sprawling on the ground aware of an indescribable stench and looking up at the cause of it.

Desmond stood there tossing his head and apparently laughing at his victory.

I knew that billy goats tended to smell but this one would've made a badly run piggery smell like good quality French perfume. As I stumbled to my feet, he compounded the act by rubbing against me.

My stomach heaved and I remember thinking that he must have been rotting from the feet up to be responsible for such a fiendish stench.

With a certain amount of difficulty, I managed to re-tether the beasts before going home.

'Phew! Where on earth have you been,' said Jane. 'You smell like a farmyard.'

'Desmond,' I muttered. 'Come and see for yourself tomorrow but for goodness sake wear some old clothes.'

The next day we arrived at the cottage and keeping a weather eye open for Desmond, inspected the anchors and chains and replenished the water supplies.

'Felicity looks pregnant,' said Jane with a woman's intuition. 'Don't be daft,' I replied. 'Anne would've told us before she left. I expect she's just got flatulence with all this grass she's eating.'

'Have it your own way but I think she's pregnant,' replied Jane.

It must have been three weeks later that I found Felicity lying on her side, rolling her eyes and her breath coming in short gasps. Panic stricken, I released her from the chain and carried her to an outhouse where I gently laid her on some straw and tried to make her as comfortable as possible.

I drove as fast as I dared to the nearest telephone box and made a call. 'I'm looking after some goats for a friend and I think one of them's dying,' I blurted out.

'What are the symptoms?' asked the vet.

'Oh... er... she's all bloated. Swollen up like a balloon and her eyes are rolling and I don't think she can breathe properly. Will you come?'

'Be right with you,' he said after I had given him the address.

I arrived back at the cottage only minutes before the vet who immediately went to the aid of the suffering nanny goat.

'Will she survive?' I asked anxiously, dreading how I would break the news to Anne.

'I should think they both will,' he replied with a laugh as he set about delivering Felicity's kid.

Mother and baby both did very well and two weeks later, Conor and Anne returned from their trip, calling in at the pub before going home.

'Hope the goats didn't give you any trouble,' said Anne. 'Are they well?'

'All three are in excellent health,' I replied smugly, handing her the vet's bill.

'Oh she's had the kid then,' said Anne, matter-of-factly. 'But did you have to call the vet?'

'If I'd known she was pregnant in the first place, I probably wouldn't have thought she was dying just before she produced and I don't suppose I would've called the vet. I expect George or Enoch would've willingly acted as midwife.'

'I didn't tell you before we went because I didn't want to worry you,' she replied.

When they left I resolved never to look after any more animals with the exception of dogs, cats and budgerigars.

'With all that space, yers ought t' keep a pig or two. Freddie, a couple 'o landlords back used ter and so did Charlie who was 'ere 'afore yous.'

'Yes m'boy. Jes t' roight spot fer 'em. Out o' ter way they'd be. Keep yers in pork 'n bacon they would. I dunno why yers doan do it. Doan cost much t' raise. Oi'll go 'alves on a young 'un wi' yers if yers loikes.'

The voice belonged to George's wife Mabel.

Were we about to hear the truth about the celebrated Dog and Partridge pigs? ...Yes we were!

We were standing in the yard which served as a car park through which people had to walk to reach the beer gardens which already housed a large chicken run and an enclosure where Flopsy and family lived.

'What's just the right spot Mabel?' I asked wondering whether she meant that I should ask the chickens to make room for a pig or two.

'Jes 'roun there. At back o' yon barn,' she replied, pointing at our bottle store and garage. 'C'mon oi'll show yers.'

I was pushed bodily through a hole in the fence and bushes, and gazed in wonderment tinged with horror at the sight. This was DEFINITELY where the pigs had been kept. There were traces everywhere.

We stood in an area of about 30 yards square, enclosed on two sides by high stone walls and by the back of the outbuildings and the hedgerow and fence on the other two.

No wonder I didn't even know the place existed; it was completely hidden from view and at first glance I felt that it should remain so.

Amid shoulder high piles of well rotted manure stood various ex-buildings. There were hovels in an equally well rotted state and in imminent danger of collapse. Timber roof supports leaned over at all angles whilst the corrugated iron and asbestos roofs swayed drunkenly in the wind that was blowing.

'You can't possibly use this Mabel. No self- respecting pig could live here.'

'We could shore up that hovel over there,' she said hopefully. 'It'd keep the wind an' rain off the animals. Tha'd be jes roight. Think of all that 'ome cured 'am 'n bacon.'

I thought of the ham and the bacon and of the luckless beasts who'd have had to provide it and made a decision, which, in the light of what I heard afterwards, proved to be the right one.

'No pigs Mabel. Sorry but I'm an Innkeeper not a pig keeper. It can't be done here lass. At least not yet. Maybe if we demolish this lot and put up some new buildings we'll think again but for now, definitely no pigs.'

Apparently, Charlie, my predecessor had tried his hand at pig rearing using advice from all and sundry as his official guide to the subject. He had been told that in addition to their usual diet, the pigs should be given beer slops which would really help them to grow.

Charlie acted on this advice and his two pigs received all the ullage from the pub on a daily basis.

It may have helped them to grow but it didn't do much for their tempers. Whoever fed them was greeted by a series of enraged grunts and snorts and more often than not, got toppled into the mire by the hungry, drink crazed porkers.

When the time came to market the beasts, it took the combined strength of four experienced farm hands to load them into the truck.

In spite of their evil temperaments, the two pigs had obviously touched the hearts of Charlie and his family because, as far as I know, once they had seen their pigs off to market, they were unable ever again to face a slice of pork or ham.

I suspect that Jane and I would've felt the same.

Behind the Bar

George had taken a great interest in the problems which we had and indeed were inflicting on the village at large, with our exuberant English Setter, Houdini.

He told us that his daughter had bought him a little dog which compared to ours was a paragon of virtue. It never barked, never attempted to escape, never caused any trouble, never chewed anything and was so well trained that, one word from him and it would sit and stay without attempting to move.

At last, Jane fell into the trap saying: 'Bring him in George, we'd love to see him. Maybe he can teach Houdini some manners.'

George went home and returned some minutes later with his little dog. Good as his word, it didn't move or make a sound. It was a beautiful liver coloured Springer Spaniel from a pottery in Staffordshire!

Wilf, Enoch and George sniggered and guffawed for the rest of the evening. We had unwittingly walked into their peculiar sense of humour and the laugh was definitely on us but we didn't have to wait too long to repay the compliment.

We now began to understand the rules of the game!

Some weeks later, George was admiring the collection of coins which were accumulating in the cracks in the old oak beam above the bar, when he reached into his pocket and producing a kidney bean, squeezed it into one of the larger cracks smirking at me, 'yers can't say yers not 'ad a bean from me.'

He cackled and grinned at Wilf and Enoch as he made his

way back to the counter. I saw my chance and took it.

'You know George, that with modern science, it's possible to grow plants without soil provided you supply enough water and nourishment for the roots to start growing. After that, all you need to do is spray the leaves with this new foliar fertilizer and apparently things grow as well as they'd do in a greenhouse.' It was a very convincing lie of which I should've been ashamed except that we had already fell victim to his one of his tricks.

Every night for two weeks when George came in, I would ceremoniously spray his bean seed with water and every night he would inspect it for signs of growth.

Then it happened.

One evening there was an excited cry from George. 'It's chitting! look just there.'

It was indeed chitting. An unmistakable little shoot had appeared. As the beer flowed, he told everybody in the bar how he had planted the bean some weeks previously and with his knowledge of modern science had instructed me in the intricacies of soil-less bean growing.

As the days went by, the bean continued to grow, producing first of all, two large leaves and then a tendril followed by more leaves until we had a very well developed plant hanging from our beam.

George was so proud of his achievement that we pinned a little plaque onto the beam next to his plant bearing the words: Planted by George of Mearsby.

Given sufficient help, word travels fast in the country and before long, the curious amongst George's acquaintances came from Rushford and the nearby villages to inspect his horticultural oddity.

Eventually the inevitable happened! Following a particularly busy night the plant disappeared. George was horrified and expressed his disgust at the sort of people who would mindlessly steal and almost certainly destroy his runner bean. I bought him a beer to console him and help him to get over the shock.

Some weeks previously, Enoch had caught me in the act of replacing a two leaved bean with one which was slightly more advanced. This was a daily chore during the growth period of the plant. Unknown to George, I had many young beans from which to choose as I had been growing them in the greenhouse especially for the occasion. Enoch was sworn to secrecy until such time as I was ready to remove the plant when he would be free to tell George the whole story.

When the time came, he did so with fiendish delight much to Wilf's pleasure and George's annoyance.

We had to give George full credit for his sense of humour as he laughingly ordered another pint and even offered to buy one for me. We drank a toast to porcelain dogs and beans in the beam.

Later that summer, I heard George telling some eager visitors about his celebrated bean plant and how it grew so well.

Enoch and Wilf were telling their listeners a completely different story.

Although our evenings had become very busy, lunchtimes with the exception of weekends and Bank Holidays were fairly quiet.

It was at this time of day that Wilf held court, free from the disrupting influence of George and Enoch who rarely put in a midday appearance.

Wilf had fought. in the First World War and never tired of relating his experiences in the trenches, of no man's land and the enemy. During one such occasion, we had a visit from Peter, an ex-German prisoner of war (1939-1945) who had stayed in this country when the war was over.

Peter was over six feet tall, built like an ox and like most big men was fortunately slow to anger.

Wilf was taking great pleasure in his story telling which was liberally peppered with words such as square heads, krauts and boche. He described British heroism, German ineptitude and generally of how he won the 'Great war' single handed.

Peter sat at the bar, impassive but inwardly annoyed.

To his credit, he refused to rise to Wilf's obvious bait but merely chatted to me about his work at the Corby steel works. For him, the European conflicts of the past were merely a bad episode in his life and were best forgotten.

Eventually he left the pub with his usual cheery farewell.

Wilf sidled up to the bar with a mischievous twinkle in his eyes and muttered through his moustache: 'Tha' were awkward. Oi'd forgot 'e were a kraut.'

The lying old toad. He'd forgotten nothing. His wartime experiences must have been responsible for the devil riding on his back and he never lost an opportunity to show his feelings for the 'enemy'.

He told us that during the Second World War, he was the mainstay of the local Home Guard as he was too old for active service during that conflict. This was yet another source of aggravation and possibly contributed to his surly demeanour.

It was during this period that he had been banned from the 'Jolly Farmers' at Rushford for unacceptable behaviour and hadn't set foot inside the place again despite the many changes of ownership during the intervening years.

'A ban's a ban,' he would say. 'An' there's still folks there as knows wha' oi did.'

One bitterly cold day in the early 1940s when an invasion was expected, Wilf was out on exercises equipped with full kit, including a rifle and a few rounds of live ammunition.

At the end of the day, frozen to the marrow, he went to the 'Jolly Farmers' to thaw himself out.

The bar was crowded with farm workers who hogged the blazing wood fire which he felt he should've been able to enjoy.

They refused to make room for him so he told them: 'A man as is foightin' fer 'is King 'n' Country ought. t' 'ave a roight t' a bit o' warm.'

They laughed and still refused to allow him a place near the fire.

'Oi'll move the buggers,' he thought as he tossed a live round into the blazing hearth.

He succeeded! The resultant explosion scattered not only the fire hogs but also the glowing embers of the fire throughout the bar.

Amongst the sea of blackened faces, there was one which was scarlet. Wilf's.

'Oi reckon as ow oi'd better be goin' now,' he said as he retreated to the door.

'And don't you ever bloody well come back!' bellowed the enraged landlord.

Wilf never did.

The front of the Dog and Partridge supported a very heavy growth of ivy or perhaps the ivy supported the 400 year old walls. It was difficult to say which.

For many years it had been Wilf's responsibility to trim the ivy when it became too overgrown.

Blissfully unaware of this tradition, I was halfway up a ladder busily hacking the plant away from the window mullions when I heard Wilf's voice from below.

'Tssch... tssch... yers doan do it loik tha'. Lemme show yers.'

I came down the ladder a bit sheepishly because I had no doubt that I wasn't doing the job properly.

Well, I was in deep trouble. Partly for not doing the job correctly but mainly for not giving the job to him.

Didn't I know that he had been the chief ivy cutter, man and boy, for the last 70 years?

He didn't give me a chance to reply.

Did something make me think that he was incapable of doing the job? Was he too old...? Did I think he was too decrepit...? I didn't want to reply.

What a dilemma. He was riding high on his pride which I didn't want to injure and as far as he was concerned, I didn't even know how to clip a hedge, let alone the ivy ...His ivy at that.

There had to be a compromise. I bought him a drink and myself some thinking time.

There was no way that I could let this octogenarian with a suspect leg and a tendency to dizzy spells to climb the ladder and thrash about with a bill hook 20 feet above the ground.

As Wilf drained his third glass, I asked him to teach me the art of ivy cropping on the basis of him as foreman and me as labourer

Fortunately, that appealed to him and he went home for his equipment. He returned with a wheelbarrow containing a huge ground sheet for catching the falling clippings. I hadn't thought of that, being ignorant of the immense quantity of ivy which would have to be cut.

He brought a long and a short handled rake for hauling out the clippings which wouldn't fall. I hadn't considered that either.

Finally he brought a set of sharpened bill hooks with handles of different lengths so that the ladder wouldn't need shifting every few minutes. Something else I hadn't considered.

All in all, with Wilf shouting instructions and encouragement, peppered with abuse, we got the job done in half the time that I thought would've been necessary.

Wilf could quite rightly say that he had once again been responsible for the annual ivy trimming and it gave him the opportunity of telling one more story to his willing band of listeners.

I paid the price when a middle aged lady came to the bar to buy him a drink and told me in severe tones: 'You should be ashamed of yourself, making an old man like that climb ladders and risk a nasty fall.' I said nothing but looked at Wilf as he stared at me with such an expression of mock innocence in his eyes that I could willingly have thrown his drink over him.

Monday night was village night when most of the locals would put in an appearance and spend the evening story telling and above all, arguing. We used to look forward, after the rush and tear of the weekend, to what we called the 'Monday night argument'.

Always at the centre of it would be Enoch, George and Wilf aided and abetted by anyone else who cared to risk the wholesale destruction of their point of view, not to mention their pride and dignity, at the hands of these three seasoned campaigners.

It was, therefore, a noticeable event when things took a somewhat different turn one Monday night.

We were visited by a Greek businessman who had been surveying the area with a view to building a factory for producing sportswear. There was a town, some 10 miles from Mearsby which he felt would be ideal for his purposes.

Enoch immediately sensed the makings of a very satisfying argument and could be seen marshalling his mental forces for what was to be 'exploited workers' versus 'the bloated capitalist' type of battle.

He wasn't to be rushed though, and wily old veteran that he was, planned his tactics and waited for the right moment.

In the meantime, the Greek gentleman introduced himself as Andreas and bought a drink for everybody including Jane and myself. He then issued a challenge to anybody willing to take him on at dominoes, the stake being a pint for the winner of each game.

The locals fell silent. They couldn't believe their ears. Here was a foreigner, in their own pub challenging them at their own game for drinks. Here was a lamb for the slaughter.

Enoch, who was one of the craftiest players in the league moved forward but was beaten into first place by George who never missed an opportunity for a free drink and who was certainly a skilled player himself.

There are many versions of the game and the first surprise came when Andreas gave George the choice. He, not unnaturally chose 'fives and threes' at which he was particularly adept. George won the first game quickly and comfortably, drained his glass and demanded his prize, saying to Andreas: 'Oi'll give yers a chance ter win a pint from us.'

The second game took a different turn. The skill born of many years practice enabled Andreas to defeat George very convincingly.

George put it down to luck and insisted on another game, conveniently forgetting to buy a drink for Andreas. At the end of five games the score was George one, Andreas four.

George was deflated. He had been mercilessly hammered into the ground on his own territory, at his own game and by a foreigner at that.

For his part., Andreas sportingly explained that he had been playing dominoes since boyhood and didn't expect George to pay for his drinks. It had all been done for the fun of it.

George readily accepted his release from the bet and offered his empty glass to Andreas for refilling, presumably as a gesture of goodwill. He also knew that Andreas' impressive roll of banknotes would more easily cover the cost of the drinks than his own slender resources.

I couldn't help thinking that things would've been different had George turned out the winner.

Andreas laughed, bought drinks all round and graciously thanked George for a pleasant and enjoyable evening.

That should've been the end of that little episode and no doubt would've been had it not been for Enoch.

His view was simple and straightforward. On a local basis, he and George were rivals and he would normally have derived great pleasure from George's downfall especially if it had been at his own hand. On this occasion, however, it was different. It was time to close ranks against the common enemy. George was no longer a rival but a close and dear friend and fellow countryman who had suffered outrageously at the hands of this stranger. To add insult to injury, this stranger wasn't only foreign but in Enoch's bigoted view, had committed the cardinal sin.

Andreas was obviously wealthy and a capitalist employer. The only way to bring this man down was by debate and he, Enoch, was a master of the art.

Carefully waiting until his glass had been replenished at Andreas's expense, he moved into action. His eyes, deep-set in his bony face, blazed with conviction as he fired his opening salvo.

'By the left. Ah s'pose that's as 'ow yers treat yers workers in yers fine factories. Beat 'em into t' ground an' then make 'em feel obliged ter yers fer their jobs. Jes loik letting George off the bet 'e lost. 'Ah bet it makes yers feel big. An' oi'll tell yers summat else. It wouldn' bloody work wi' me.'

'Oh Hell.' I thought, he doesn't want an argument, he wants a fight and he must be 30 years older than Andreas.

He glared implacably at his adversary, his hat which never left his head, pulled firmly over his knitted brow. His jaws were tightly clenched and his gnarled forefinger stabbed the air in front of him, challenging Andreas to reply.

With a grin which nearly split his broad face in half, Andreas rejoined. 'Enoch, I do believe that you're a communist!'

That was about the most unwise thing that anyone could have said.

Enoch, fiercely independent, and a strong believer in the rights of the working man, was certainly no communist.

There followed the most bitter and acrimonious argument that I had ever heard. No mercy was shown on either side but as it didn't look as though they'd come to blows, everyone settled down to enjoy it.

Closing time came and went. Doors were locked, lights dimmed and still the argument continued and still the drinks flowed until at midnight, I rang the huge brass bar bell and called a halt declaring it a drawn contest.

The following evening, Enoch slid up to the bar and whispered: 'That Greek wallah. 'E were roight about the way 'e does business but oi weren't gonna side wi' 'im.'

'You and George are crafty old devils,' I said. 'You only bought one drink each all night.'

Laughing, he said: 'By the left. You're learning boy. You're learning. There's three people as won last night. You, me and George an' t' silly bugger as lost doesn't even know it.'

...Was there no end to Enoch's trickery?

'The trouble with Mearsby,' said the well dressed, well spoken, middle aged man. 'Is that it's totally lacking in community spirit.'

'Nobody seems to care about anything except themselves,' interposed his equally well dressed, well spoken wife.

I couldn't believe my ears.

They felt that the village needed some form of social committee and a community centre. As far as I was concerned, they had one. It was called the Dog and Partridge.

They wondered if we could spare a room where they could organise Ladies circle meetings and other gatherings where local people could meet to discuss village problems.

I was astounded. They didn't even live in the village and rarely visited the pub, yet here they were proposing that they should somehow organise the social life of the village.

Enoch, without saying a word was taking a keen interest in the conversation and I could tell by the expression on his face that he didn't like what he was hearing.

The couple chatted with me for about an hour and it transpired that they had been instrumental in setting up regular social meetings under their guidance in other local villages but in their own words, 'had never been able to do anything for Mearsby'.

'Arrogant, misguided busybodies.' I thought but kept my own counsel. From what we knew of Mearsby, the last thing that local people needed was interference in the way that they ran their lives and certainly didn't need anybody doing things for them.

The couple finally suggested that I attend a meeting that was to be held in Rushford so that I could speak about Mearsby, how it had changed and what could be done to strengthen its community.

I agreed to attend, having seen the encouraging look on Enoch's face and knowing that he must have had something up his sleeve.

Mr and Mrs Swift left the pub in what appeared to be a triumphant mood.

Enoch cursed on his way to the bar where I stood reflecting on my recent conversation with the Swifts.

'By the left, we'll bloody fix 'em,' exploded Enoch, waving his gnarled and bony forefinger at me. 'Bloody lousy interference. They've bin at it fer bloody years an' its toim as 'ow they were stopped.'

He was clearly upset so I looked him in the eyes for a moment and quietly said: 'If there are sides to be taken, then I'm full square behind you and the village.'

He called a council of war and within a few minutes Wilf, George, Enoch and I were huddled together in the private corner of the pub.

It was there in the glow of the log fire, that we designed our grand strategy for the preservation of the anonymity of Mearsby. It was worked out in great detail.

I was to give the talk to the people of Rushford and surrounding villages and expound the view that small rural communities do not change in themselves, the indigenous population changes very little and very slowly and that the centuries old way of life in a place like Mearsby is something to which other communities might try to aspire.

I was to elaborate that what is seen on the surface bears little resemblance to the true working of the community and above all that outside influences would most likely be damaging to the delicate substance of good neighbourliness by interfering with the existing social structure of village life.

That was to be the general essence of the talk.

It was never given because Enoch felt that if the flavour of the talk was leaked to the Swifts, then my invitation to speak would be withdrawn ...how right he was.

Two days later, I received a telephone call from Mrs Swift who was terribly, terribly apologetic but she had made a mistake with the number of proposed speakers. As I was the last to be asked, would I mind awfully standing down on this occasion and that I would be remembered for the future.

'I bet I will.' I thought and chuckled to myself as I put the telephone back in its cradle. Victory was complete and we'd certainly celebrate that night.

I received no further invitations to speak and no approaches were ever again made on the subject of a community centre.

The Swifts continued to visit our pub occasionally, looking presumably for signs of a community spirit.

I often wondered if they ever looked deep enough to see any.

If you live in a small village, you'll know that giving help and indeed, receiving it isn't a calculated act. It's not something that needs organising. It's simply a way of life.

Certainly, the people of Mearsby didn't need to publicise and be recognised for services performed on their neighbours' behalf and in fact went out of their way to ensure that their good deeds were kept as private as possible. You can be sure that a kindness never went unreturned.

Money rarely if ever changed hands, and this is where the people of Mearsby and I am sure, many tiny villages like it, differed from many of their urban counterparts.

People never quantified what had been done for them and always returned a favour within their own capabilities.

Wilf came into the bar one evening with what, to him, was a major financial problem. He had too much cash lying around the house because he had been out when the various traders called for settlement of their weekly accounts and he was worried in case he was burgled over the weekend and lost it.

It really was preying on his mind so I sealed up his money in an envelope and put it in my safe to re-assure him.

As far as I was concerned, that was the end of the matter until Wilf needed his cash.

The following lunchtime, he came into the pub by the back door where nobody could see him, slyly gave me a heavy shopping bag, winked at Jane and sloped off to the bar where he sat in his favourite chair as though nothing had happened.

We found that the bag contained about 10 pounds of freshly dug parsnips together with a quantity of different vegetable seeds to set the following Spring.

That was Wilf's quiet, almost secretive thank you for looking after his money.

It was quite typical of the Mearsby way of life where people looked after each other as a matter of course.

No wonder that Enoch was so against what he saw as outside interference especially against the backdrop of his own charitable activities.

He would've been mortified had it been widely known that his assertive and outspoken character actually masked a very generous and sympathetic nature.

'They were t' days,' laughed Enoch.

'S'right Dad, there's not many as can say they were born in the dead centre of town loik I was eh?' remarked his son, Jim.

Enoch, unable to miss an opportunity to have a go at Jim

quickly replied: 'Naw son an' oi'll tell yers summat else. The way you're goin' it won't be long afore yers back there what wi' yers drinkin' an' late nights an' all.'

With his usual lack of deference Jim immediately responded. 'Yous a roight one t'bloody talk. It doan seem t' ha' done yous any 'arm an' oi doan think as 'ow yers ready t' go back there yet!'

'Alright you two,' I cut in. 'Can't you talk about anything without arguing. Come on let's hear the story.'

They were talking about the time, just after the Second World War when Enoch got a job with the local Council as a caretaker in the Rushford cemetery where his duties included grave digging.

Jim was born in the lodge next to the cemetery gates and was the youngest in the family which included four girls. These girls were, to Enoch, understandably the finest daughters that a man could have wished for and he lavished upon them all his fatherly care, guidance and above all protection.

When his eight year old Julia came indoors and reported a man and a woman fighting on a wooden seat near the railings, he rushed to investigate.

What he saw didn't shock him; he had been in the Army too long for that but it did infuriate him.

'There they were,' he said. 'In my graveyard, on my bench makin' love loik it were goin' out o' fashion. Loik bloody rabbits they were. It may ha' bin dark but moi little girl had seen 'em an' oi weren't 'avin' tha'! Oi knew 'ow t'bloody fix them two an' oi crep' away quiet so's they wouldn' hear me.'

Back at the lodge, he hatched his plan with Edna who was

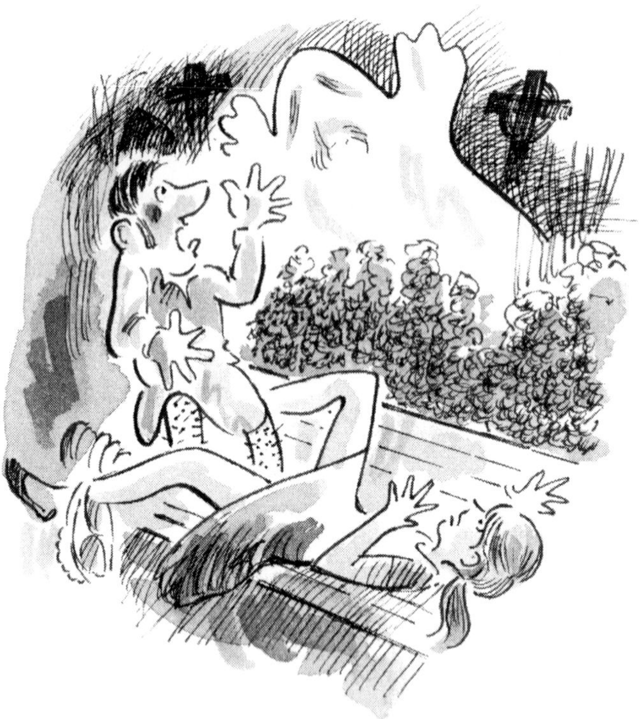

all for going out with a rolling pin and a bucket of cold water but Enoch had something much more subtle in mind.

In the dark and especially when it was a bit misty, as it was on this particular night, the graveyard was an eerie place. You wouldn't necessarily expect to see a ghost but if you did you would be convinced and no doubt frightened out of your wits.

Enoch crept soundlessly, armed with a white sheet and a long swishy birch twig to the couple who were still otherwise engaged. Silently he drew the sheet over his head and took up position behind a laurel bush close to the bench which was within easy reach of his birch switch.

With a flicking motion, he touched the back of the man's neck.

No reaction. He tried again. The man loosed an arm and slapped the back of his neck as though he was being troubled by a mosquito.

'Got yers... yers buggers,' thought Enoch as he twitched the birch twig again and at the same time let out a low moaning sound. The man turned his head and at that moment, Enoch leapt, swathed in white, above the laurel bush, a bone chilling wail leaving his throat, looking and sounding for all the world like an avenging wraith.

This was too much for the man.

With a gasp, he was off the bench and away pulling up his trousers as he rushed, stumbling through the gravestones in his headlong flight from the horrible apparition.

The young woman, now alone, took one look and fell unconscious on the bench, a scream of terror dying on her lips.

Enoch, panic stricken ran to the lodge shouting 'Mother', his pet name for Edna. 'Mother yous got t'help me. You'd better come quick, oi think oi've bloody killed her.'

'If yous aven't, oi reckon oi will,' she replied but agreed to see what she could do.

In the event, when they returned to the bench, the woman had gone, obviously recovered from her faint.

'Tha's t' last toim oi reckon as they'll gerrup ter their tricks in front o' little girls,' said Enoch, with a great deal of satisfaction in his voice and as far as he could tell, it was.

Enoch raised his empty glass to the assembled and fascinated audience and before long it was full of his favourite brew. 'Aye, oi'l tell yers, we ad some fun down there.'

'Tell 'em about Sedgewick the solicitor, Dad. Tha's a good story,' chirped Jim. 'By the left. Hold yers noise boy. Ah'l tell it when ah'm good 'n' ready,' snarled Enoch.

He was ready a few minutes later when he had drained his glass and offered it for a refill. Half a dozen eager hands reached out for it, such was Enoch's story telling power.

'Ah now lemme see. 1948 oi think it were or were it 49. Never mind... Old Sedgewick, 'e were a big name then, came 'n saw me. All worried 'e were 'bout this job 'e wanted doin'. Y'see 'ed got this burial as 'ad t'go down in t'family tomb tha' was loik, wha' would yers say, overcrowded already.'

Enoch told him that it was impossible.

'There's no choice in the matter, Enoch, it's got to be done this way,' said Sedgewick. Enoch had noticed the desperation in his voice.

'Can't be done... t'bloody hole's too full already.'

'It has to be done Enoch. It's in the will. Look, perhaps this will help,' said Sedgewick offering £10 to Enoch.

'Might be able t' do it. No. No. it's bloody impossible.'

'Would this make it easier?' said the worried solicitor offering a further £10.

£20 in 1949 was a great deal of money to a Council worker with a wife and five young children to support.

'It'll go down orlroight. It can be done wi' a struggle. Where there's a will there's a way,' quipped Enoch.

The next day, he started digging.

'18 bloody inches down an' oi 'it t' bloody top box,' he told us.

'Couldn' drop another box on top an' oi'd taken 'is flamin' 20 quid.'

Enoch was lucky. Although the graves were very close together, the one on which he was working had a narrow path alongside but as he couldn't dig up the path, he had to excavate underneath it by digging diagonally from the grave and then straight down.

'Nigh on bloody impossible wi' a shovel. Oi'd 'ad t'crawl in t' 'ole wi' a trowel an' coal shovel an' burrow away loik a flamin' mole. Oi then 'ad t' shore up t' flamin' path so's it didn' collapse 'n' send t' vicar down there wi' t' box. Oi were puttin' t' finishing touches t' it when t' flamin' cortege came in through t' gates 'n' oi 'ad t' run loik 'ell t' fetch me cloak fer t' interment.'

He got back to the grave side in time for the burial when the solicitor caught his eye and gave an approving nod. Enoch's fists were tightly clenched under his cloak as he sweated out the ceremony, waiting for the coffin to be lowered.

'Nice'n gentle now. By the left. Doan tip it wha'ever yers do,' he thought.

'An' then it slid down tha' 'ole as easy's though oi'd oiled the sides. Just enough room but it made it. We were all 'appy. T'old lady bein' buried got 'er last wish, owd Sedgewick got 'is money's worth 'n' oi got 'is £20 but tha' were t' last toim oi tried a trick loik tha'.'

'Yes.' I thought. 'Knowing you Enoch, it's the only one you're prepared to tell us about.'

'By the left,' he cried. 'Thirsty work this story tellin', thirsty work indeed. There was a few shallow ones in them days,' he went on. 'But tha's another story an' oim as dry as a bone.'

During one of her shopping trips to the nearby town of Rushford, Conor's wife, Anne had met the local vicar's wife and took the opportunity to ask for information about biblical stories. Her two young sons, Sean and Seamus had been attending their Sunday school and having shown a particular interest in the story of The Good Samaritan, had wanted to look it up in The Bible and read it for themselves. Anne had no idea where to find the passage and naturally thought that the vicar's wife would be the ideal person to ask. Unable to give the reference from memory, she promised to contact Anne with the relevant information.

A week later, returning from town, Anne's car broke down,

so, with heavy shopping bags and two little boys in tow, she set about walking the remaining two miles to her remote cottage. A half mile further on, a car drew level with the struggling woman and stopped. The window was wound down and the vicar's face appeared as he declared in his best clerical voice: 'Ah my dear, the reference you're seeking is: Luke 10. Good morning to you.' With that he drove off. Suddenly his brake lights came on and he reversed back to Anne, the boys and their mountain of shopping. The significance of The Bible reference must have struck him somewhat belatedly since he opened his car doors and drove them all to their home in a heavily embarrassed silence which was only broken by Anne's slightly sarcastic comment: 'Thank you vicar, I'm sure you'll receive your reward in heaven.'

Everybody has an 'off-day' from time to time when everything they try to do goes wrong. Normally two such events in one day are enough to make you think that someone, somewhere has got it in for you but when the whole day is an absolute disaster from the moment you leave your bed in the morning until the moment you return to it at night, then you're entitled to feel downright demoralised. What you're about to read is the true story of one man's battle against unknown forces in an effort to try and retain his sanity and self control during a period of one day. That man was my brother Charles and to make matters worse, it was his birthday.

Waking at six o'clock, he was aware that something was wrong. He felt cold and damp. A thunderstorm was in progress and the window above his head was wide open. He was cold and damp because the wind had been blowing the heavy rain straight through the open window onto his bed, the top of which, whilst not awash, was soaked through. Miserably and cursing aloud, he got up and went for a hot bath to counteract the effects of the wet bedding. Leaving the bath taps running, he went back to his bedroom. He never did get the hot bath which he expected as the old coke boiler which supplied our hot water must have gone out during the night, for, when he returned to the bathroom, cold water was streaming from the hot tap leaving the tub three quarters full and totally cold. Nothing much happened for a couple of hours after that and no doubt he thought it was just a bad beginning to what would be a normal day. He was wrong... Horribly wrong.

It was our beer delivery day and since the opening of our cellar, we had been lowering the barrels down through the unusual entrance by a somewhat clumsy system of wooden ramps and long restraining ropes. It had always been a little precarious because it only needed one rope or one piece of wood to slip and the heavy barrel would've crashed down the stone steps into the bowels of the cellar. The draymen, whose responsibility wasn't over until all the beer was safely on the thralls were horrified when they saw our method of lowering barrels and demonstrated to Charles a somewhat rougher, but altogether safer way of doing it. The two draymen simply tied the rope to the handles at the top of the barrel and bumped it down the makeshift wooden ramp to the cellar floor. With all the 18 gallon barrels safely down, Charles said: 'OK lads. Thanks for your help but I can manage the little ones by myself. See you next week.'

The 'little ones' to which he had referred were nine gallon kegs of lager weighing in excess of 100lbs each. These were cylindrical containers having a steel collar welded onto their top and bottom making them look rather like depth charges. Tying the rope to one of the collars, he took the strain on the rope and eased the keg onto the ramp. With a sound like a whipcrack, the keg and its collar parted company resulting in nine gallons of lager hurtling down the steps and coming to rest with a crash against the barrels below and Charles falling backwards into a large bucket of ullage which soaked him in stale beer from the waist down. 'Bloody Hell,' he cried in anger. 'A right bloody day this is turning out to be.'

But there was more to come. Much more. The boiler had been fired by this time so Charles went, smelling like a brewery waste pipe, for his long overdue bath. He came back in his fresh working clothes saying,: 'I'll go and vent those barrels now.' 'Be careful,' I warned. 'They'll be a bit lively in this humid weather especially after the keg hit them. I'll come down with you and give you a hand.'

Holding the peg and mallet at arms length, he firmly vented the first barrel. To our surprise, there was no sound of escaping gas and no foam issuing from the vent hole. 'Strange,' muttered Charles as he leaned over the barrel to examine the vent. With the force of a cork leaving a Champagne bottle, the head of hops which had been blocking the vent hole struck him right between the eyes followed by a cloudy stream of partly fermented beer which like a geyser, sprayed directly up at him completely soaking his fresh, clean shirt. I fell about the cellar floor racked with almost hysterical laughter. 'Happy birthday,' I spluttered. 'Have that drink on me.' Ignoring me, he stormed out of the cellar and up to the bathroom leaving me to complete the venting which I did without further mishap.

A little later he took the car into town to buy a few odds and ends expecting to be gone for about an hour. Two and a half hours later, George walked in, his face split in a roguish grin, followed by Charles who looked far from happy, covered as he was, with thick mud.

Apparently, on his return from town, his car had skidded on a bend and had ended up with the rear wheels firmly stuck in a ditch. He had called George to pull it out with the tractor but somehow in the process had slipped into the ditch which, because of the heavy rain from the morning's thunderstorm, was full of slippery mud, most of which appeared to be stuck to his clothing. 'Thanks for your help George,' glowered Charles as I bought him his pint. 'I don't think anything else can happen to me today. I think I've had everything that's coming my way.'

But he hadn't. Not by a long chalk.

'Why don't you take Houdini for a run this afternoon Charles,' suggested Jane. 'You should be out of harm's way in the fields and you'll be able to calm down and relax a little.' 'Right,' he replied. 'Whatever's happening to me, I'll get it out of my system.' They returned sometime later, both soaked to the skin. Houdini, naturally was unconcerned but Charles was almost gibbering with rage. 'Your bloody dog! I'll kill him... I'll bloody murder him so help me! I never want to see that piece of canine filth again!'

After yet another hot bath, he explained that Houdini had bolted, as he often did, and after a long chase had finally allowed himself to be captured at the edge of the brook where, just as Charles was fastening his lead onto the collar, the dog had tried to bolt again catching Charles off balance and toppling him into the stream.

'In the circumstances and especially because it's your birthday, you'd better not come behind the bar tonight. Just enjoy yourself and mingle with the others,' I said. 'Thanks,' he replied. 'I think that might be for the best.'

Whilst he was sitting at the bar that evening, the lager barrel emptied and he offered to go down to the cellar to put a fresh barrel online. 'No!' I said. 'We're not taking any chances. I'll do it myself.' I must have tried to hurry the job because before I had managed to plug in the valve properly, I received a jet of high pressure lager in the face and chest.

I returned, dripping, to the bar where Charles started falling about with laughter. Waving his arms about, he knocked over a pint pot of Guinness which cascaded down his jacket and over his trousers. With a show of dignity which I never realised that he could possess, he rose from his stool, paid for a replacement pint for the unfortunate Guinness drinker and strode away from the bar. His last words that day were: 'I think that's enough for anybody. Goodnight all!'

The customers who watched him go couldn't understand his strange behaviour.

Tracy was a very impressionable young lady. She wasn't terribly bright but by the same token, she wasn't stupid or she would never have been taken on by Jane to help with the kitchen work. She was married to Frank and lived not far from the pub in a little row of Council owned cottages near the church. Unbeknown to us at the time, Frank had been in trouble with the police some years previously for losing his temper with one of his peers and had beaten 10 bales out of him which culminated in a charge of GBH of which he was found guilty and served his time accordingly. We never had a problem with Frank who was a model customer and in fact was always willing to lend a hand during our busiest periods. It didn't occur to me at the time that our regulars were quite frosty towards him because of his past, of which we had no idea, but occasionally I did feel that there was something smouldering beneath his otherwise shy but friendly surface.

Frank worked on a shift basis for a transport company so he could be at home during the day, absent all night and vice-versa.

Tracy was bored during the evenings when Frank was away so she agreed to help Jane with the cooking and general kitchen duties whenever she was required. This suited us well because in a tiny village like Mearsby it wasn't easy to find reliably available people to help out at peak times.

One of our regular patrons was a young man called Michael who was a self employed freelance electrician. He was quite a handsome chap, single, earning good money and lived at home with his widowed mother. He used to visit the Dog and Partridge once or twice a week, have couple of pints of County Ale and then leave. Keeping himself to himself but a friendly enough soul, he went largely unnoticed by our regular throng.

Talk about being thick! We hardly noticed that Michael was visiting us much more regularly and especially on the nights when Tracy was on duty. He would stay for the entire evening, drinking far more than usual and then sit chatting at the bar with Tracy until closing time, long after the kitchen was closed. At closing time he would say: 'I'd better escort Tracy to the cottage 'cos its dark now.' Off they'd go and Jane and I thought nothing more about it. The villagers of course knew far more than we did.

How Frank found out about the affair that Tracy was having with Michael, we do not know but he did. Leaving his work unexpectedly early one night, he arrived at the pub at about 11 o'clock almost foaming at the mouth in his anger. We tried to calm him but he was having nothing of it. I began to understand the depths of violence seething in this otherwise placid chap.

He stormed away from the Dog and Partridge towards his cottage swearing, cursing and muttering some rather unholy things. Totally unaware of the drama about to unfold, we closed-up and went to bed.

Something must have alerted Michael to his impending

doom because he leapt naked from the bed he was sharing with Tracy, grabbed and pulled on his underpants and threw himself out of the upper floor bedroom window onto the flower bed below just as Frank slammed through the front door and charged up the stairs like a demon from hell. To his eternal credit, he didn't lay a finger on Tracy despite his temporary derangement. He found another way to take his revenge.

In the meantime, Michael, semi-naked, had driven away from the cottage and taken refuge in the countryside to escape Frank's wrath. In fact, as it turned out, he stayed hidden in the woods until he returned to his mother's house at about six o'clock the following morning.

At about two o'clock that same morning, Michael's mother had been rudely awakened by an insistent banging on her front door. Reluctantly she had answered and was horrified by what happened next.

Frank screamed at her: 'Here's your son's clothes and his woman's clothes,' hurling them up the passageway. ' And here's his other baggage,' as he threw his naked wife headlong into the house. Without another word he left.

We can only imagine the conversation that Michael had with his mother when he arrived home at six o'clock in the morning.

There was no sign of Tracy or Frank, or indeed, any sign of life at their cottage for days after the event. The Police were called in and having interviewed Michael and his mother, they understood that Tracy had left their house almost immediately following Michael's return.

Our friend Ron declared that he was convinced that there

was no foul play apart from what everybody in the village knew by this time, but that we'd have to be interviewed on an official basis.

Ron declared an interest, i.e. our friendship, so we were interviewed by the new brash young police sergeant from Rushford.

'You realise that Frank is quite capable of murder don't you,' said the sergeant. 'So I need to ask you some questions to help us further our enquiries.'

One question that stuck in my mind was, 'This relationship with Michael. Was it Plutonic?'

My only reaction was, 'No sergeant, it was a little more Mercurial than that.' The jibe went straight over his head. 'Thank you Mr Roberts that's most helpful,' he replied. Perhaps his response went straight over my head.

The sergeant was absolutely convinced that Frank had murdered Tracy and a team was sent in to dig up the cottage gardens. Needless to say, this was one of the most exciting things ever to have happened in Mearsby and equally needless to say, Tracy's remains were not found.

Three months later, just as I had opened the bar one evening, I received a tearful telephone call from Tracy. She was stranded on the A1 trunk road just outside Peterborough. Jane and Charles manned the bar and I drove to pick up Tracy. I could hardly believe my eyes when I saw her. She was dressed in only shorts and a T-shirt, both of which were covered in greasy hand marks in all the wrong places. Feeling very sorry for her but absolutely stuck for words, I drove her back to the pub.

'Right my girl, It's a hot bath and a change of clothes for

you followed by a decent meal and then if you're up to it, you can tell us what the hell has happened.' I blustered.

It transpired that she had literally run away from Michael's house on that fateful morning and joined a travelling circus that was heading north. She had been treated very well by the circus folk and had been well fed and watered in return for looking after some of the animals.

Her worst experience had been hitch-hiking back down the A1 when a lorry driver who couldn't be described as a knight of the road had decided that she wanted something more than a ride home.

Inevitably she and Frank separated and later divorced.

When the embarrassment had passed, Michael returned to the pub one evening when he was presented with a toy parachute by the regulars!

Crime and Disaster

Running a remote country pub and meeting a complete cross section of society somehow tunes your senses. Some people you accept immediately whilst others take a little longer before you feel comfortable with them. Others start alarm bells ringing in your head the moment you meet them.

Our pub was situated not far from the Duke of Gloucester's family seat and at the time, there was great concern about their security against terrorist attack. It was well known that the local and county police were in a state of high alert to avert such a possibility. We had all been asked to keep an eye open for anything out of the ordinary which may have raised our suspicions.

One lunchtime, we were visited by two gentleman who we had never seen before. That in itself was nothing new because we often saw strangers. These two however, made me feel very uneasy. They had London accents but were dressed in Tweed jackets, checked shirts with woollen ties, brown drill trousers and sturdy leather shoes.

Despite their brave but vain attempts of camouflage as countrymen, they actually stood out like sore thumbs.

Engaging them in conversation, I was surprised to hear that they claimed to live in a town not 10 miles from Mearsby.

They were very curious about our growth in business and where most of our customers came from. They wanted to know when we had our busiest nights and were generally very insistent for information about the area.

My worst suspicions were confirmed when I asked them about Alan, the landlord of the 'Fox and Hounds', the most popular pub in their town. They told me he was fine and that the business was going from strength to strength.

By this time, the alarm bells were ringing so loud that I knew they were not genuine. There was a 'Fox and Hounds' but there certainly was no Alan at the pub in question.

They had finished their beers and were about to leave when I asked Jane to look after the bar whilst I slipped out to the kitchen to make a private telephone call.

Fortunately Ron was on duty at the local police station when I made the call and he quickly came to the telephone.

I gave him a full description of the two and told him that they were about to leave. He was extremely grateful for the information and told me to do nothing. He would see me later.

That evening, and off-duty, Ron came to the pub and asked to have a quiet word with me. Apparently the local police had apprehended the two suspicious characters on the road between Mearsby and Rushford a full five minutes before the County police had arrived on the scene.

I was delighted. Not only had we been instrumental in the arrest but the police had acted swiftly enough to collar them before they could carry out their crime.

I was thinking in terms of all the publicity we'd get when he brought me down to earth with a bang.

'Well spotted Nick. You've obviously got an eye for the bad guys. They were on local detachment from Special Branch helping to protect the royals!'

As you can see, life in the country wasn't all milk and honey and the potential for crime and unpleasantness was still there, but in a tiny community like Mearsby, the scope was limited to incidents such as domestic quarrels and poaching. When something out of the ordinary did occur, the whole village was aware within minutes and the incident would be magnified out of all proportion to its importance.

One Saturday night, just on closing time, Mabel, who was a little nervous at the best of times, burst through the door looking as though she had just seen a ghost. She was close to tears and it took a drop of brandy and a few minutes of soothing before she was able to tell us what had happened.

'E' were there... lookin' at me. 'Orrible e' were... Big black beard an' 'uge eyes starin' through t' window.' She took another gulp of brandy. 'Oi were jes gettin' ready fer bed an' e' stood there leerin'. Yes. Tha' were it. Leerin' an' sort o' grinnin' e' were.'

We established that the prowler was scruffy, tall, bearded and had been in Mabel's front garden about five minutes previously.

'Roight lads,' said Tom — the village's strongest man who was renowned for his ability to lift the rear end of a bullock off the ground if the beast refused to move. 'Le's get after 'im. We can't 'ave our women froightened by a bloody peepin' tom.'

I didn't give much for the prowler's chances if Tom caught up with him and decided to call the police.

That of course presented me, as a publican, with certain problems, the most obvious of which was that I had a pub full of people still drinking after time with the police on their way. I had no idea whether Ron and Cyril were on duty or not.

I knew most of our customers quite well and after a brief word to explain the situation, they quickly drained their glasses and left.

There had to be an exception and one small group refused to cooperate and deliberately slowed down their drinking.

Normally, I would've taken a hard line and they'd have left but poor old Mabel was still in a state and I didn't want to subject her to an angry scene so I simply opened the door to Houdini's quarters and let things take their natural course.

A true guard dog would've snarled and growled but not Houdini who didn't have an ounce of aggression in him.

Full of goodwill, he leapt, his five stone bulk landing squarely on the lap of one of the recalcitrants and with one mighty swish of his tail, cleared the table of its glasses and proceeded to lick and paw his way through the group who, after 20 seconds of that treatment, capitulated and hurriedly left.

Houdini had his uses after all!

In the meantime, a posse of villagers had formed and on instructions from Tom, were splitting off into smaller groups in pursuit of the prowler.

Apart from Western films, I had never seen anything like it.

Reminiscent of a lynch mob, they were armed with torches, pick axe handles and ropes, looking for all the world as though they'd tear the man apart if they caught him.

The police arrived a few minutes later. 'I think your first job will be to stop the mob.' I said, explaining what was happening.

A short while later, the disappointed villagers returned on instructions from the police, to the pub, where we were unable to serve them anything stronger than coffee.

A thorough search was coordinated by the sergeant in charge but nothing was found and the decision was made to abandon the activities until the following morning. I have no doubt that, in their mood, the villagers slept with loaded shotguns beside their beds.

Early the following morning, Jane saw a tall scruffy looking man with a beard walking past the kitchen window and heading towards Mr Ford's farmhouse. Immediately, we telephoned the police and within a few minutes, after a short chase, the prowler was arrested and taken away for questioning much to everybody's relief.

It turned out that the man was a harmless tramp, known to the police and as it happened, to many of the villagers, and had simply been looking for a suitable shed or barn in which to sleep for the night.

Mabel's fear and exaggerated story had triggered off the villagers' protective instincts and could have had some serious consequences if the police hadn't acted so swiftly but all had ended happily although it did illustrate to me the depth of feeling which these people had for their community.

The tramp was never again seen near the village.

Mrs Catchpole, who lived quite alone in a small cottage not far from George and Mabel's was one of the most elderly residents of Mearsby and like most of her contemporaries was a fiercely independent person who lived solely on her old age pension but was helped, like many others in the village by Enoch's quiet but regular donations of firewood, eggs and vegetables.

Her strict Victorian upbringing was reflected in her attitude to those around her and in particular to men.

She allowed herself only one visit a week from a neighbour and if that neighbour happened to be a man, then he wouldn't be allowed in the house unless there was another woman present presumably to protect her ageing virtue. Apart from the weekly visit, when no doubt food supplies would be delivered to her, she had no contact with the outside world.

She was clearly contented to be left alone with her thoughts and memories except when she was visited by her sole relative, a niece who would bring her to our pub where they'd sit for hours in front of the fire and drink two milk stouts apiece. Without fail, on these occasions, she would pay for a pint of bitter for George and Enoch with a quiet and dignified insistence which gave neither of them the opportunity to refuse despite their feeble attempts to do so. For all her independence and hermit like existence she recognised that their unselfish assistance made her life a little more comfortable than it would otherwise have been and was determined to show her appreciation if only with a pint or two.

George, observant by nature, had noticed that there had been no smoke curling from Mrs Catchpole's chimney for a couple of days and had heard no sound from her cottage during that time.

Fearing the worst, he looked through the downstairs windows but saw nothing. His wife, Mabel, was out at the time and, being aware of Mrs Catchpole's fear or dislike of men in general, he approached her front door with some trepidation. He knew that the back door was always barred and bolted against intruders. Banging loudly on the old brass knocker, he yelled: 'Is yers there Mrs Catchpole?' There was no reply. 'Is yers orlroight Mrs Catchpole?' Still no reply.

Swallowing the lump in his throat because he was rather fond of the old widow. He yelled: 'If yers doan answer me this toim, oi'll break yers bloody door down an' come in after yers'

To his relief, a feeble voice replied: 'Doan yers dare come 'n 'ere alone. Oi'm not well but oi'll be orlroight.'

He looked through the letter box but all he could see in the darkened room was a foot sticking out behind the door which opened onto the staircase.

Not wishing to upset her anymore by barging into her house he cried: 'Yer stays where yers are. Oi'll go 'n' get Mrs Brent t'come 'n' see yers.'

Mrs Brent was a very calm and capable woman to have around in an emergency. She returned almost immediately with George and a key to the cottage where they found poor old Mrs Catchpole lying at the bottom of the stairs after falling from the top step. An ambulance was called and within the hour she was being treated in the District General Hospital.

Luckily for her, George was an observant and insistent character because she was found to have broken her hip sustained from the fall some 48 hours previously.

The operation was a great success and she became as fit and healthy as ever but still maintained that streak of independence and pride which had stopped her from screaming for help when she needed it most and which was very nearly the end of her.

Unknown to her, following the accident and her return from hospital, she was watched like a hawk by all her neighbours.

Late one morning, I was returning from a shopping trip in Rushford when I saw a column of smoke rising high into the clouds.

'Some poor devil's got a fire on his hands.' I thought as I turned into the lane that led to Mearsby.

As I drove closer, I could see a deep red glow at the base of the smoke and realised that it was a very serious fire and that it was coming from the village... My village.

'Not the pub.... Oh please God not the pub.' I prayed as I put my foot down and roared towards the blaze.

It wasn't the pub but Mr Ford's farmyard which was only about 150 yards away from the Dog and Partridge

Apparently, someone had been welding and a stray spark had ignited some straw and very quickly spread to the barns and other outbuildings, growing so rapidly that it was out of control within minutes.

I changed my clothes and rushed to the farm to see if I could help but there was nothing to be done.

All the stock of sheep and expensive Charolais cattle had been moved to safety and the fire brigade was there in force doing its best to limit and contain the fire. They had no chance of putting it out.

The villagers were milling about unable to do much except watch the blaze and consider what might have happened had there been a strong breeze blowing.

Enoch's voice could be heard above all the noise. 'C'mon down son, yer'll get bloody roasted. Yers bloody fool. C'mon down.'

It was the first time that I had seen Enoch show a real concern for his son Jim who was on top of a hayrick, hosepipe in hand. He leapt around the stack, which wasn't alight, like a Red Indian doing a rain dance.

'Oi'm on bloody spark watch,' he cried back. 'And there's enough bloody hot air coming my way to roast me anyways.'

Enoch took the point and found himself another vantage point.

I returned and opened the pub. A short while later, smoke blackened from his efforts, the senior fire officer came in and said: 'Two pints of bitter please and somewhere to hide. I don't want to set an example to the men.'

I gave him his beers and put him in the private snug bar.

Eventually, a group of thirsty firemen came in to the pub and asked for beer and a quiet place to drink it as they didn't want the boss to find them.

'Stay in the bar...' I told them. 'You'll be safe enough here. I know he's far too busy to worry about you being in the pub.' I don't think that any of them ever realised what had happened.

The damage to the farm was enormous but thankfully, nobody was hurt and no doubt the cost of repairs and replacements was met by the fire insurance.

The following day, the village electricity supply was turned off so that overhead cables which had been close to the flames could be examined and tested, This was clearly very necessary but at the same time very awkward as our catering equipment was powered by electricity.

At lunchtime we had a visit from two strangers who wanted a hot meal.

'I'm sorry but we can't help,' said Jane. 'The power has been cut off.' 'Has it now,' said one of the strangers as they drank their beer and left. A few minutes later they returned, grinning from ear to ear.

'Steak and Chips for two please,' said one of the men. 'You'll find you've got power for the next half hour or so,' said the other.

They were right!

The two electricity board engineers enjoyed their meal, said their goodbyes and left. A short time later the power was cut off again.

The farm fire was the talk of the village for quite some time. George was explaining to Wilf, the extent of the damage to buildings and machinery, the upheaval caused, the difficulties which Mr Ford would have with the continued smooth running of the farm and the many thousands of pounds which would have to be spent on repairs and replacements.

Wilf responded by tapping his blackthorn stick on the floor to make his point. 'Could be yers roight. All ah knows is it's put me 'ens orf the lay.'

That to Wilf's way of thinking was the single most important effect of the blaze, although he did add: 'Ford were lucky to get 'is Kale eyed cattle out.' I sniggered but George guffawed. 'Doan be a bloody owd fool. Them's not Kale eyed, them's Sherry laced cattle.'

Nature rarely gives us mere mortals a great deal of warning when she intends to stage one of her spectaculars and so it was on that Friday evening when the hurricane struck Mearsby.

It had been a fairly normal evening. Wilf was up to his usual trick of browbeating people into playing bar billiards with him and then winning nearly every game he played although not always through superior skill. Usually he would make a 'mistake' with the scoreboard and increase his lead by a few hundred points. His opponents might have looked in amazement but, as Wilf was so open about it, nothing was ever said and when they got to know his tricks, they'd often adjust their own score accordingly.

Another of his habits was to poke the coal and log fire with his blackthorn walking stick. "Ardens it up', he would say.

This particular evening, he fell asleep in his favourite chair and awoke to find his stick a foot shorter than when he had started out. Cursing under his breath, he got to his feet and shuffled off home, his passage through the darkness lit by the small hand torch which he carried.

I calculated that he had only just reached the safety of his cottage when it all started.

A tremendous rumbling and roaring announced the beginnings of a storm. The first squall which hit us must have struck almost vertically downwards as the smoke from the fire belched from the chimney in thick clouds throughout the room.

'Bloody good job Wilf weren't sittin' there then,' laughed Enoch. 'Tha' would 'a' got t' owd bugger movin' a bit sharp.'

The room was cleared of smoke as quickly as it had been filled when the back door burst open under the force of the raging wind as it whipped itself up into a frenzy, tearing tiles off the roofs and hurling them around the village as though they were playing cards.

George, whose bladder dictated his movements to a large extent had no choice but to go out through the back door and disappeared into the gloom. A piece of flying tile or something had put our rear floodlight out of action. He returned a few minutes later looking shaken but clowning as ever with an empty window frame wrapped around his shoulders. 'Nigh on bloody crowned me. Oi'd jes taken a few steps across t' yard when t' bloody thing came crashin' down behin' me an' there's broken glass everywhere. 'An tha's no' all.'

'On t'way back t'bloody wind picked me up 'n' if oi 'adn't grabbed t' bloody gatepost 'n' hung there flappin' loik a bloody windsock oi reckons as 'ow oi'd a bin blown all t'bloody way ter Rushford. An' oi reckons as ow yers bloody chickens 'a' bin blown orf their roosts Nick. But doan worry, it'll be orlroight... You'll see. It'll be orlroight.'

Grabbing a torch and donning a thick coat, I ventured out into the darkness.

The chickens hadn't been blown off their perches but were hanging on with grim determination as the gale roared through a gaping hole in the planking which had once formed a wall of the hen house. Leaving them to it as there was nothing that could be done in the storm and darkness, I struggled against the screaming wind back to the house where I saw the rough hole in the wall left by the window frame which had so nearly brought an untimely end to George.

He had only exaggerated a little.

That wind was strong enough to lift a man off his feet and bowl him down the lane. Before I reached the shelter of the doorway into the pub, I heard, above the shrieking tumult of the hurricane, the sound of timber being torn apart and the screech of tortured metal followed by an almighty crash.

It wasn't until the following morning that we discovered what had happened.

Back in the bar, we had to turn up the volume of the music to try and make it heard above the thundering reverberations of the vicious North Easterly as it cleaved its way through the village, vandalising everything in its path. It was well after closing time when the wind moderated to a reasonable gale force and people felt confident enough to start their journeys home.

Just before one o'clock, Jane and I got to bed and lay there wondering what we'd find when the morning came. As we slept, the wind died away.

The sun rose out of a clear sky and heralded a calm, bright day in total contrast to the violence of the previous evening when we thought that the pub, if not the entire village would be torn apart.

Reports started coming in on the extent of the damage and that miraculously, nobody had been hurt.

There must have been divine intervention because the amount of debris, including tiles, bricks, baulks of timber and glass which had been catapulted through the village had to be seen to be believed. It looked as though Mearsby had been subjected to a mortar attack.

A chimney on Enoch's cottage had been blown down, taking part of his roof and most of the out house with it. Not one cottage had escaped damage. All had tiles missing and most had at least one broken window. Rubble and broken glass lay everywhere.

The almighty crash I had heard the night before was a hovel roof in our ex-piggery being wrenched from its uprights. That roof was corrugated iron measuring 20 feet by 15 feet and was found twisted but pretty well intact over 50 yards away in Mr Ford's farmhouse driveway. The wind had lifted it over a 10 foot high wall and carried it like a giant wing until it crashed into the trees lining the drive. The trees bore the scars for many years and I tremble to think what would've happened had it hit somebody in full flight.

The operation to clean up the village got underway immediately and, as expected, everybody set to with a will working in small teams.

By nightfall, all the older folks' cottages had been temporarily repaired and made weatherproof and not a trace of debris remained in sight but it took a few weeks more to restore the village to its pre hurricane condition.

If our old friends the Swifts had ever needed proof of community spirit, they'd have done well to have visited the village in the aftermath of that disastrous hurricane. Perhaps then, they'd have realised what a true sense of neighbourliness was all about. That evening in the pub Wilf's only comment, grumbling as ever, was: 'If it's not a bloody fire, it's t'bloody weather. It's put m'bloody 'ens orf t' lay again.'

Enoch laughed. 'By the left. There'll be enough firewood down t'keep us all goin' fer months.'

Walter rubbed his hands together. 'I reckon as 'ow there'll be enough buildin' work t' last me roight through t' winter.'

I reflected. 'It's an ill wind that blows no good.'

Last Orders

We had reached a stage with the Dog and Partridge where we were unable to expand the business further without major alterations to the building. It had got to the point where the bar serving area was too small to cope with the expanded business. The kitchen was too small. They desperately needed to be enlarged.

The old barns in the car park were ripe for renovation and would've made a fine site for a licensed restaurant to complement the traditional old pub.

All of this would've cost a considerable amount of money.

Unfortunately and sadly, the brewery showed little enthusiasm for financing the project and we certainly didn't want to borrow money to invest in structural improvements to a building that didn't belong to us despite the fact that it would've increased the turnover of the business.

It had become increasingly difficult to sustain the level of business with the facilities at our disposal and I suppose to some extent, we had become victims of our own success.

We looked at the possibility of moving to another pub but the only places within our price range tended to be run down and in need of the sort of work that we had put into the Dog and Partridge.

We really had no choice. We'd stay put and muddle through until we could find some acceptable way of acquiring or raising the necessary cash at the minimum risk to us.

Life has a funny way of taking unexpected twists and turns and whilst we were pondering our future at the pub, I received a telephone call from an old friend in the Healthcare business which had been my career prior to moving to Mearsby.

In short, I was made an offer that I couldn't refuse. This position would lead to a senior management position in Asia but I wasn't to know that at the time.

After a lot of soul searching, we decided to sell the tenancy of the Dog and Partridge and rejoin corporate life.

It wasn't an easy decision but it was to lead to unlimited world travel and a beautiful home in the mountains above the city of Taipei in Taiwan, Republic of China for nearly nine years, The stories from the Orient are fascinating and formed a wonderful episode in our lives. Despite the agony of leaving Mearsby and its wonderful characters, we wouldn't have missed it for the world.

For Jane and I, running our own country pub and moulding it into the sort of place that we wanted, was one of the most satisfying projects that we've ever attempted, and crowned with a feeling of achievement, it was a highly rewarding way of life too.

As a warning to would he licensees, I would advise that the work is very hard indeed but if you attack it with a sense of purpose, you'll enjoy every minute. There is a great deal of fun to be had and a great many interesting people to talk with provided you take the trouble to listen to them.

Whether you want it or not, you're appointed as counsellor, friend and confidante and these are positions which you must take seriously because a careless word from you could destroy a marriage, break up a family or even worse.

Good ideas and schemes which pay dividends, the long summer days when all is right with the world and you're so busy that you do not know which way to turn can be offset by the grip of an icy-cold winter when you begin to think that your business will fail.

When things look bleak, you must keep on trying and smiling regardless of how you feel inside.

There is nothing more likely to destroy a pub than a miserable licensee and wife.

At our leaving party which packed the place to capacity, we challenged our friends to drink the place dry. They very nearly succeeded. It was during this party that I learned a secret from Enoch after I told him how much we had enjoyed our tenancy at the Dog and Partridge.

Waving his boney forefinger at me, he replied: 'By the left, boy. Ah knows wha' yers means an' oi'll tell yers summat else too. It were great fer me too when oi were landlord o' this very pub more'n 20 years ago!'

I stared at him in disbelief. 'It's true boy... Oh yes... Them wer' t' days. Ah remember when owd...'

But that's definitely another story.